*"Tom Glavine is the most strong-minded individual I have ever been around. He has an unparalleled knowledge of the game of baseball, and a work ethic to match. Tom is a combination of class and street toughness with a NEVER-GIVE-IN attitude. Tom is consistently excellent. That's his standard."*

Leo Mazzone, pitching coach with the Atlanta Braves

# Baseball
## for
# Everybody

# Baseball for Everybody

## Tom Glavine's Guide to America's Game

### Tom Glavine
#### with Brian Tarcy

CHANDLER
HOUSE
PRESS

Worcester, Massachusetts
1999

*Baseball for Everybody: Tom Glavine's Guide to America's Game*

ISBN 1-886284-43-1
Library of Congress Catalog Card Number 98-89737
First Edition
A B C D E F G H I J K

Published by
**Chandler House Press**
335 Chandler Street
Worcester, MA 01602
USA

**President**
Lawrence J. Abramoff

**Publisher/Editor-in-chief**
Richard J. Staron

**Director of Retail Sales and Marketing**
Claire Cousineau Smith

**Editorial/Production Manager**
Jennifer J. Goguen

**Book Design**
Anna B. Type & Graphics

**Cover Design**
Marshall Henrichs

Chandler House Press books are available at special discounts for bulk purchases. For more information about how to arrange such purchases, please contact Chandler House Press, 335 Chandler Street, Worcester, MA 01602, or call (800) 642-6657, or fax (508) 756-9425, or find us on the World Wide Web at www.tatnuck.com.

Chandler House Press books are distributed to the trade by
National Book Network, Inc.
4720 Boston Way
Lanham, MD 20706
(800) 462-6420

# Dedication

**I WOULD LIKE TO DEDICATE** this to my parents, Fred and Mildred Glavine for their unending support in and out of baseball, and throughout my life.

# Table of Contents

## Part 4 – The Show, The Major Leagues

# About the Authors

**TOM GLAVINE**, a two-time Cy Young Award winner, is the most successful left-handed pitcher of the 1990s. Devastatingly consistent and smart, he has dominated by daring batters to bring their best against his best. He is a four-time twenty-game winner and a six-time All-Star who, more than anything else, is a winner. Tom knows the game of baseball. As a member of the strongest pitching staff of the decade, the Atlanta Braves, Tom has appeared in seven National League Championship Series and four World Series during the 1990s. In 1995, he was named World Series MVP after shutting down the powerful Cleveland Indians with a one-hit performance in the Braves 1-0 Game 6 title clincher.

Tom Glavine is more than just a great pitcher. He is a great all-around athlete who was drafted by the Los Angeles Kings of the National Hockey League. But Tom chose baseball. He has become one of the most dominant hurlers in the game while he has quietly and professionally raised

money and awareness for a variety of good causes. He is a dedicated volunteer to the National Sports Committee of the Leukemia Society of America. He has also been an invaluable fund-raiser and contributor to the Georgia Council on Child Abuse. As the honorary chairperson of this organization, Tom plays host to "Field of Dreams," a celebrity golf tournament in Atlanta to benefit victims of child abuse. Tom also initiated a program to benefit the Georgia Transplant Foundation called "Spring Training," where fans compete with professional athletes at games such as pool and ping pong. Tom's generosity was recognized when he received baseball's Roberto Clemente Award, which is given to players who best exemplify leadership and a willingness to be goodwill ambassadors for baseball.

**BRIAN TARCY** is a freelance writer and book developer living in Falmouth, Massachusetts. He is the author or co-author of ten books including collaborations with former Boston Bruins superstar Cam Neely; USA Olympic Hockey champions Katie King and Tricia Dunn; and ESPN analyst and Super Bowl champion quarterback Joe Theismann. Tarcy has written for several newspapers and magazines. He is a graduate of Ohio University in Athens, Ohio. He is waiting, patiently, for the Cleveland Indians to win the World Series.

# Other Great Sports Books from Chandler House Press

## Golf for Everybody:
### *A Lifetime Guide for Learning, Playing, and Enjoying the Game*
by Brad Brewer and Steve Hosid
with a Foreword by Arnold Palmer

## Hockey for Everybody:
### *Cam Neely's Guide to the Red-Hot Game on Ice*
by Cam Neely with Brian Tarcy
with a Foreword by Bobby Orr

## Gold Medal Ice Hockey for Women and Girls
by Tricia Dunn and Katie King
*Members of the Gold Medal-Winning*
*1998 U.S. Olympic Women's Ice Hockey Team*
with Brian Tarcy

Visit us online at www.tatnuck.com

# Acknowledgments

**THE AUTHORS WOULD LIKE TO THANK** a number of people who helped us along the way, especially Dick Staron, publisher and editor-in-chief of Chandler House Press for dreaming of this project and giving us guidance. We would also like to thank Jennifer Goguen, editorial/production manager at Chandler House, for her tremendous efforts to pull this together. And we want to thank Anna Botelho of Anna B. Type & Graphics for her great graphic design. Betty Shaughnessy of Atlantic Edtek Typing gave us accurate transcriptions of our conversations. We want to thank Chris and Rita Hamilton for most of the great photographs that appear in this book. We would also like to thank Kim Parsons of Woolf Associates and Michael Snell of the Michael Snell Literary Agency for their great help and representation.

**TOM GLAVINE** would like to thank my parents Fred and Mildred Glavine for their love and support, and I would like to thank my brothers, Fred

and Michael, and my sister, Debbie, for their love and support as well. I would also like to thank my wife Chris for her love and support. I would like to thank my little league coach Jim Bowley for his early teachings, my high school coach Jon Sidorovich for his guidance as I grew and developed, and all my coaches in the Atlanta Braves system for teaching me and molding me into the pitcher I have become. I would also like to thank all the teammates I've had throughout my career. My success wouldn't have been possible without them.

**BRIAN TARCY** would first like to thank Tom Glavine for your friendship, guidance, and professionalism in this process. We talked baseball, it was great. I learned a lot and I had fun learning it. But in 1995 I watched from TV land as you had the best game of your life and dominated my favorite team. I futilely cheered against you. So here's what I (can't beat 'em, try to get 'em to join) say now: I think your life would be perfect if only you pitched for the Cleveland Indians. C'mon Tom, just think about it when you are a free agent again. I'd give you my Rocky Colavito baseball card if you signed with the Indians—well, you'd have to sign for more than one year.

I want to thank my father and brothers for playing baseball with me, and my Mom for being my Mom. Every time I throw a baseball, I go back to Lyndhurst. And, obviously, I need to thank the usual gang: Wally Sigler, Paul and Heidi Perekrests, Seneca and Martha Anderson (hey Seneca, someday the Red Sox will win—Indians first though!), Vaughn Sterling, Gregg Alexander, Jason Rutledge, and Miles, Morgan, and Tristan Anders. And, I want to thank Joe Theismann, Cam Neely, Katie King and Tricia Dunn for teaching me so much about sports before I started this project. I admire winners and you taught me a lot.

I want to dedicate this to every kid I ever coached or coached against in Falmouth Little League. You guys are the best.

But as for the Cleveland Indians—Just once. C'mon, please! But I want to thank John Hart—as a long-suffering Indians' fan, I would've never believed it possible.

I just want to add one thing to five people: my best friend Maureen Anders; and my four children, Denim, Derek, Kayli, and Marissa—you are my reason.

# Introduction

**I KNOW THAT BASEBALL IS FUN FOR EVERYBODY.** I also know that there is something profoundly American and civic-minded—athletic yet distinctly academic—about baseball. Professors and historians write about it. It must be important.

I am just a baseball player. I am not the judge of importance. But as a player I know how baseball works, so I decided to write about it right now, while it is here and fresh in my mind. I am a pitcher—present tense. I know enough to be successful and I have tried to teach you how in this book. But just like everyone involved with the game, I will always be learning.

Despite the homage paid to the game by the intellectuals and literati, I decided to present baseball with a different twist. Unlike those esteemed witnesses and former players who have watched the current game from afar and written with eloquence, I thought I could offer something new.

I have written about baseball because I love it and I want to share my knowledge with you. It is a great game and I know a lot, but no one fully understands it. Baseball is mystical, and baseball is perfect.

So grab a hot dog and a cold drink—that's what you do at baseball games. Put on the hat of your favorite team (if you can't decide, I suggest the stylish Atlanta Braves), and turn the page. It's time, as the umpires say, to "Play ball!"

# Where Were You When History Happened?

PART ONE

**IN AMERICA, TIME HAS ADVANCED AS IT HAS IN MOST CIVILIZATIONS.** But in America, we have the best way to measure time. We call it baseball.

As a player of the greatest sport that could ever be invented in the next thousand millenniums, I know that I tread on the hallowed ground of legends including Babe Ruth, Jackie Robinson, Willie Mays, and Sandy Koufax. I've pitched against Mark McGwire and Sammy Sosa. My teammate is Greg Maddux. History always happens. That's why I decided to begin this book on the hallowed ground. It is, after all, the foundation of the game.

# The Great American Drama

CHAPTER ONE

**WHERE I GREW UP**, this is what the great-grandfathers say: *I'd like to see the Boston Red Sox win the World Series just once in my lifetime.*

Baseball is a game of stories. As a player, or as a fan, I know that the stories, the comparisons, and the connections to our days on earth are what lifts baseball above other sports. Red Sox fans wait for a championship because they've been waiting for so long. So they keep waiting and hoping, and still another summer goes by. That's baseball—a great way to keep track of time. I've heard the old folks talk—recreating pitch-by-pitch dramas that eventually broke their hearts. When they talk, they become younger versions of themselves. You can see it in their faces. They go back there.

I certainly can recall certain moments in baseball history. I grew up right outside of Boston. I remember glorious and tortured snippets from years and Octobers past. My playing career, in many ways, is a continuation of

when I was a kid cheering for the hometown team. New triumphs make up for old wounds. In baseball as in life, time always goes on. I now have the luxury to be part of the story.

**Baseball is more than a sport, it is a great story.**

© Chris Hamilton, Atlanta, GA

As much as I used to root for the Red Sox, I am an Atlanta guy now, part of some new incredible dramas (more later). But when I think of baseball drama outside of my own career, I think of Red Sox moments. No matter how old you get, baseball is a game of youth. The moments I remember, and the stories I was told, come from Boston.

The saddest for Red Sox fans, of course, is the story of the greatest baseball player ever, Babe Ruth, who helped the Red Sox win their last championship in 1918. One year later he was sold to the New York Yankees so the owner of the Red Sox could have enough money to stage a Broadway Show called *No, No Nanette*. Some say Ruth put a curse on the Red Sox. There's lots of evidence.

Then there was that horrific day in 1978 when Bucky Dent of the New York Yankees hit an improbable home run in a one-game playoff to beat the Red Sox and advance, eventually, to the World Series. One year the New Englanders pinned their hopes on the irrepressible Jim Lonborg, the brainy right-hander who had the bad luck to run into the only person who could have beaten him in October 1967—a hard-throwing, cold-blooded competitor named Bob Gibson. In that World Series, Gibson's St. Louis Cardinals beat the Red Sox in seven dramatic games.

Baseball books start with this stuff because it is lore, history. I start with it because I grew up in Billerica, Massachusetts—right outside of Boston. We grew up wounded to the essence of our New England spirit yet absolutely enthralled by the thought that somehow *in our lifetime* the Red Sox will win it all.

Gosh, the stuff we've seen. In 1975, the Red Sox lost to the Cincinnati Reds in the greatest World Series ever played using a script that was surely written by some higher power. All Red Sox fans went from the top of the emotional mountain to the bottom in a mere twenty-four hours. Like all Red Sox moments from my youth, it was a roller coaster that eventually became a free fall.

And then there was 1986. I was already a professional baseball pitcher in the Atlanta Braves system. Yet some things are in your blood. When the Braves didn't play, I rooted for the Red Sox. That year, every year—even this year. When I am not playing, I still check the scoreboard and hope they win. But in 1986, they came to within one strike of winning the World Series against the New York Mets. Then, like a predictable house of cards, the whole dream collapsed. It was excruciating, as hits piled upon walks

When the baseball rolled through first baseman Bill Buckner's legs in 1986, Boston Red Sox fans braced themselves for more of the heartache that has followed the team since Babe Ruth was sold by a greedy owner in 1918.

AP / Wide World Photos

and errors and mental mistakes—baseball's version of the Chinese Water torture: drip-drip-drip until suddenly the dam burst in the form of an easy ground ball through the first baseman's legs and the New York Mets were suddenly alive again. One game later, the Mets were the champions. In New England and across the world, fans watched as the television showed the tortured faces of the Red Sox players juxtaposed with the ecstatic body language of the champion Mets. It was real drama being played out by real human beings. Nobody was acting.

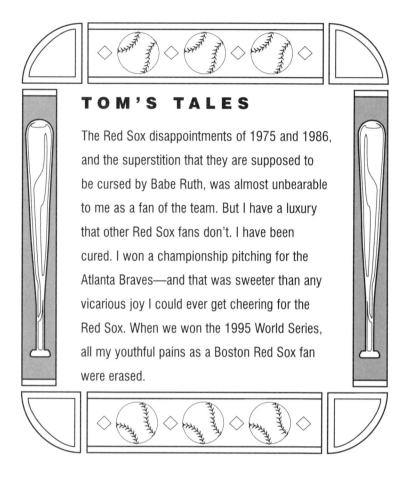

### TOM'S TALES

The Red Sox disappointments of 1975 and 1986, and the superstition that they are supposed to be cursed by Babe Ruth, was almost unbearable to me as a fan of the team. But I have a luxury that other Red Sox fans don't. I have been cured. I won a championship pitching for the Atlanta Braves—and that was sweeter than any vicarious joy I could ever get cheering for the Red Sox. When we won the 1995 World Series, all my youthful pains as a Boston Red Sox fan were erased.

And still the great-grandfathers dream. Everyone born in New England after 1918 says the same thing. Just once. That'd sure be some story.

Of course, now I say this: They could always become Braves' fans.

## *Rebirth—Sunshine and Spring Training*

For baseball players and fans, life begins in February. After a long winter of other sports and other stuff, when players change teams either through

trades or free agency (more later), teams begin to assemble in the warm weather of Florida and Arizona for a six-week exhibition and tryout season called spring training. After all that *nothingness*, suddenly there is baseball again. It is green and warm.

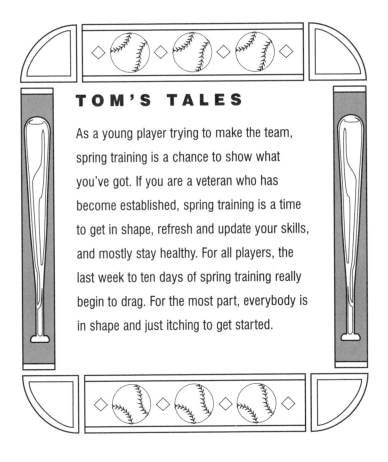

### TOM'S TALES

As a young player trying to make the team, spring training is a chance to show what you've got. If you are a veteran who has become established, spring training is a time to get in shape, refresh and update your skills, and mostly stay healthy. For all players, the last week to ten days of spring training really begin to drag. For the most part, everybody is in shape and just itching to get started.

Of course, it has a specific purpose—*training*. Players can try as hard as they want to stay *in shape*, but there is still something different about *baseball shape*. For instance, no matter how much running a player does, the movement required to field a ground ball is different. You get sore muscles. You need to develop those muscles again. As a pitcher, I throw off of a mound starting on January 1, but it changes when I begin facing batters. Suddenly, I have to take it up a level—both mentally and physically. Before, I was just trying to throw strikes. It's a different story when you are suddenly trying to get a batter out. Of course, I have a different focus now than when I first came up. I don't need to make the team. I need to get myself in shape and build up my endurance so that when the season starts I am 100 percent healthy and ready to go.

© Steve Babineau

Spring training is a time when every player and every team expect to have the best year ever.

Spring training is about optimism. Last year is history. Every team has been retooled a bit and every player offers plenty of logical reasons why they are due to have the best year of their career. All baseball players dream of greatness. In spring training that is magnified because so many have *a chance*. By the time spring training rolls around in the last weeks of February, winter has dragged on for too long and all true baseball aficionados are itching for some news about competition. Players want to compete. There is a skip in everyone's step because as illogical as it may

seem in the middle of winter, baseball's heart begins to beat. The summer sport unfolds like a great novel, and spring training (which technically begins in winter) is the introduction.

## The 162-Game Story

It is a cliché but it is true: Baseball is a marathon, not a sprint.

The season lasts 162 games—from the beginning of April to the beginning of October. Essentially, teams play every day. A bad game is followed by … another game. A good game is followed by … another game. If you win three in a row or lose eight in a row, there is always another game. It goes on and on. And, inevitably, teams win games and lose games. All teams. All teams seem to generally win and lose at least sixty games. That leaves about forty games up for grabs. Generally, a great year for a team is when they win 100 or so games and lose sixty or so. A horrible year is when they lose 100 or so games and only win sixty or so.

Forty games.

The 1998 New York Yankees won 114 games, and my team, the Atlanta Braves, won 106 games. So, think about it. Even if you have a great year, you have bad games. The season is too long and the competition too intense. The same is true in reverse for bad teams. They do win games. I know about both. Early in my career I was on some really bad teams that actually won games, and I have been blessed to recently be on great teams that, despite it all, have lost games. Players are the same. Even in the years when I have won the Cy Young Award, I've had bad games. Baseball is like that. The best hitters, those who hit for a .300 average (more later), fail 70

percent of the time. But it's a long season. Those three out of ten hits stand out over 162 games. Believe me, I want a guy like that on my side.

## The Old Heroes Matter Right Now

When a modern baseball player such as Mark McGwire or Sammy Sosa does something great, he does it within the context of history. There is no finer way to measure a sport, and no sport has the rich history of baseball. Mark McGwire and Sammy Sosa became *The Story* of the 1998 baseball season precisely because Roger Maris and Babe Ruth created earlier benchmarks in the same category—home runs.

The accomplishments of players from the past help give modern feats some sort of perspective. The reason Cal Ripken received so much publicity when he played in his 2,131st game in a row was because Lou Gehrig had played 2,130 games in a row back in the 1920s and 1930s.

### HOW IT HAPPENED

Baseball has been around almost as long as the United States of America. Some say that Abner Doubleday of Cooperstown, New York invented the positions in 1839, and others claim that Alexander Cartwright of New York City created a set of rules that closely resemble baseball in 1845. In either case, it was a young nation that first started playing baseball.

Baseball players chase numbers. Numbers come from the past.

# *Jackie Robinson and America*

The game is now played between the best baseball players in the world. Prior to 1947, major league baseball was played between the best *white* baseball players in the world. Jackie Robinson, the first black baseball player in the major leagues, changed that. Now there are players from all over the world playing in the major leagues.

Jackie Robinson of the old Brooklyn Dodgers also changed America.

Jackie Robinson is an American hero.

If Martin Luther King Jr.'s premise was having a dream, then I believe that Jackie Robinson lived the first part of the dream. He paid a huge price and never complained, but he broke through and, along with Larry Doby of the American League's Cleveland Indians, pioneered the mix of greatness that is modern baseball. But he was so much bigger than baseball. In the 1940s, the only major team sport in the country was baseball. It was the country's athletic stage and Jackie Robinson forced every person who followed the sport to notice that talent and drive are colorblind. He simply dominated. And many players hated him—stories of the horror he endured during his first years in the league are epic. But he played baseball and never fought back—no matter how hard it was to stay calm, he did. He was a great baseball player.

Jackie Robinson is seen across America in a context much bigger and simpler than baseball. People are people. That's how I see it. He is as much of a national hero and legend in the struggle for equality as Martin Luther King Jr. His stage was certainly as big.

## Sudden Death – Playoffs and Pressure

After the 162-game marathon, it becomes a series of sprints. If you can win three sprints, you get a trophy.

The first sprint is a five-game playoff series: The first team to win three games gets to go to the next round, the League Championship Series.

The League Championship Series is a seven-game playoff series: The first team to win four games gets to go to the World Series.

The World Series is a seven-game playoff series: The first team to win four games is the champion and they get a trophy. Actually, baseball has a lot of trophies, but this is the only one that really counts.

That's how it works, briefly, but the truth is that it builds. Game by game, day by day—there is increasing pressure. More is on the line. There is a cliché in baseball that players who lose playoff games go home to play golf. And players really don't want to go golfing. In the playoffs, the difference between winning and moving on, or losing and going home to golf, is not much. It may only be one run after seven games. It can hurt. It

can really hurt. But we do it because we know that there is a chance that we can be up by one run, too. And nothing feels better.

Baseball is a pressure cooker because there is always something on the line. Even in a game between bad teams late in the year, there is something on the line. Players have careers. Contracts come up (more later). This is business. It is also competition, and you can never underestimate the value of competition to professional athletes. I have never met a professional who does not burn for it. And in baseball, it burns back in the month of October. That's the month of sudden death—or sudden golf.

## Yogi Berra Was Right— It Really Ain't Over Until It's Over

The great catcher for the New York Yankees of the 1950s, Yogi Berra, is famous for saying things that don't seem to make sense until you think about them. One of his most famous sayings about baseball is, "It ain't over until it's over." At first, you think, *of course*. But actually, basketball games and football games and hockey games are often over before they end, because there is often no chance for a team to catch up within the time remaining.

Baseball has no time clock.

Baseball has innings. And if a team is on offense, it doesn't run out of chances as long as it keeps doing well. That's baseball. No matter what the score is, it ain't over until it's over.

# *Eyeball to Eyeball in the Seventh Game*

A World Series lasts seven games, if both teams win three games first. Then, it's down to one game. It happens. I've been there. I've cheered for it. It is chilling.

The pressure to perform at that point is greater than anything you can imagine. The world is literally watching. When there is a seventh game, it is do or die. The doorstep is right there—ultimate victory or almost. The difference is gigantic. If you have been in this position before, your experience helps you through the game; and you can remind yourself that the things you could do in July will work in October, too.

As a fan, or even as a player who is not playing, it is much more difficult. In those cases, I believe, the only thing you can do is rely on faith or superstition.

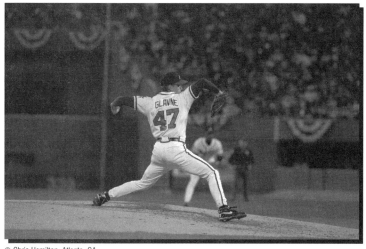

© Chris Hamilton, Atlanta, GA

**When I pitched the final game of the 1995 World Series, I tried not to think about the pressure.**

# Why We Still Talk About It: Babe Ruth to Mark McGwire

## CHAPTER TWO

**THERE IS A LINEAGE OF HEROES IN BASEBALL.** Babe Ruth was once the Paul Bunyan of this American sport; now we have Mark McGwire. The beauty of the connection between these two great athletes is that their accomplishments, though some seventy years apart, are remarkably similar because they inspire awe. The only difference is...

I never saw Babe Ruth. You probably didn't either. Mark McGwire and Sammy Sosa are as close as we are going to get. We are lucky. But baseball fans of every era are lucky because they witness unique accomplishments by talented players. Fans and players talk about old games and players because they astonish us. Baseball, in many ways, provides a historical continuum that we can all relate to.

There will never be another Babe Ruth, another Mark McGwire, or another Sammy Sosa. Of course, there will never be another Joe

DiMaggio, Bob Feller, or Jackie Robinson, either. And the list goes on and on and on...

Baseball is more than just names from the past. Everybody can play baseball. Though not everybody can play major league baseball—and only a few become legendary—everybody can play baseball at some level, which is one of the essential and great things about it. You don't have to be seven feet tall to play baseball. You don't have to weigh 300 pounds. You just have to know how to throw, catch, hit, and run. Your size doesn't matter as much as your skill and your heart. Your background doesn't matter at all. Baseball is America's game—everybody is equal.

What follows is a mere overview of baseball history, from my perspective, and I know it is incomplete. But that's okay. It is meant to provoke discussion. So, what do you say? Who would you start with?

## *I Remember Yaz*

I start with Carl Yastrzemski, the left fielder of the Boston Red Sox who won the Triple Crown (RBIs, Home Runs, and Batting Average) in 1967, while leading his team to an improbable American League Championship. He was my favorite player when I was a kid. He was a local legend around Boston—a great player and a good guy who did everything the right way. That may be the most important thing for any baseball hero to do—to reach his peak when his greatest fans are kids. I think we remember our childhood heroes forever and a day.

# *Twenty from the Past*

Baseball has a rich history. Here I list a few essential names so you can argue about who I left out.

- **Babe Ruth**—He was the most mythic of all sports heroes. In the 1910s he was a dominating young left-handed pitcher for the Boston Red Sox. In the 1920s and 1930s he became the greatest power hitter ever for the New York Yankees. He had perhaps the most famous season ever when he hit sixty home runs in 1927. He finished his career with 714 home runs.

- **Lou Gehrig**—The Iron Man first baseman played his career alongside Babe Ruth to create the most devastating batting order in baseball history. Once when he replaced Wally Pipp at first base, he played 2,131 games in a row.

- **Branch Rickey**—As the general manager of the Brooklyn Dodgers, he signed Jackie Robinson as the first black player in major league baseball.

- **Jackie Robinson**—This brilliant Hall Of Fame ballplayer was the first black major league baseball player. Robinson broke the color barrier in 1947 when he joined the Brooklyn Dodgers. He played with fire but responded to hatred with restraint.

- **Roberto Clemente**—A tremendous athlete with a rifle for an arm in right field, Clemente of the Pittsburgh Pirates was one of the best all-around players ever. He was also a tremendous humanitarian who

died in a plane crash while bringing relief aid to earthquake victims in Nicaragua.

• **Ty Cobb**—For twenty-four seasons, mostly with the Detroit Tigers, this high-intensity—some say mean—player dominated. He finished his career with a lifetime .366 batting average.

• **Rogers Hornsby**—One of the greatest second basemen ever, Hornsby won six batting championships in a row, and a total of seven. He batted .424 in 1924 for the St. Louis Cardinals.

• **Bob Feller**—Some swear that this hard-throwing right-hander of the Cleveland Indians was the fastest pitcher of all time. He was certainly dominating and he showed a flair for the dramatic by throwing a no-hitter on Opening Day of the 1940 season.

• **Lou Boudreau**—He was a player-manager who started managing the Cleveland Indians at age twenty-four. In 1948, the shortstop batted .355, hit eighteen home runs, and had 106 RBIs while leading his team to a world championship.

• **Willie Mays**—He was an exciting player for the New York Giants and San Francisco Giants who played a dominating center field and provided tremendous offense with both power and average. He finished his career with 660 home runs and is considered the best ballplayer ever by many who saw him play in the 1950s.

• **Joe DiMaggio**—From his mythic fifty-six-game hitting streak to his ten pennants and eight world championships in thirteen years, to his marriage to Marilyn Monroe, DiMaggio was larger than life. This

New York Yankee center fielder put up great numbers and he did it all with class.

• **Ted Williams**—he wanted to be known as the greatest hitter of all time and any Boston fan can tell you it was true. So can any other fan. Williams, who hit .406 in 1941 (the last time anyone has hit over .400) finished his career in fitting fashion by hitting a home run.

• **Bob Gibson**—He was an intimidating pitcher who overpowered batters in the 1960s for the St. Louis Cardinals. He had one of the greatest years ever when he finished with a 1.12 ERA in 1968.

• **Satchel Paige**—Leroy "Satchel" Paige was a tall, lanky pitcher in the Negro Leagues of the 1930s and 1940s. He had a blinding fastball and an engaging personality. He finally got his chance to pitch in the major leagues when he was in his forties, making him the oldest rookie ever.

• **Josh Gibson**—A catcher in the Negro Leagues before Jackie Robinson broke the color barrier, Gibson never played in the major leagues. If he had been given the chance, some say he could've been the greatest ever. One of his many legendary feats is a 580-foot home run that he hit at Yankee Stadium.

• **Sandy Koufax**—The word to describe Sandy Koufax's brief career is "dominating." From 1962-1966, he had an unbelievable 111-34 record with 100 complete games for the Los Angeles Dodgers.

- **Reggie Jackson**—Best known for smacking three home runs in Game 6 of the 1977 World Series, he earned the nickname Mr. October by continually performing when the games counted most.

- **Brooks Robinson**—The most spectacular third baseman in the history of the game, he won the Gold Glove Award for the best fielder at his position every year from 1960-1975. This Baltimore Oriole was a great big game player.

- **Hank Aaron**—He holds the all-time record for home runs in a career, 755. The ultimate player for the Milwaukee and Atlanta Braves, he could hit for average as well as power. He won three Gold Gloves, too.

- **Nolan Ryan**—He has the most strikeouts of any pitcher in the history of baseball—5,714. Ryan, who pitched for the New York Mets, California Angels, Houston Astros, and Texas Rangers, was a dominating performer until he retired at age forty-six. Most impressive, perhaps, is the fact that he threw seven no-hitters.

## Ten from the 90s

The story continues, and the game continues to produce great players. Here are a few who have flourished in the last decade.

- **Roger Clemens**—Five Cy Young Awards and counting for Rocket Roger, who has an intimidating fastball and an incredible work ethic.

- **Greg Maddux**—He is a brilliant pitcher with pinpoint accuracy who forces batters to swing because he is always around the plate. He has won four Cy Young Awards and continues to dominate. I love having him as a teammate.

- **Dennis Eckersley**—This recently retired relief pitcher started his career as a starting pitcher and spent the second half as a dominating closer. He had a flair on the mound and devastating stuff.

- **Barry Bonds**—He is an incredible left fielder who produces as well as any player in history on offense. Bonds is the complete player.

- **Tony Gwynn**—This prolific hitting machine can sometimes do anything he wants with a bat in his hand.

- **Andres Galarraga**—He is a great defensive first baseman with incredible power. He is an RBI machine.

- **Ken Griffey Jr.**—Some compare Griffey to Willie Mays. He is the complete package—a great athlete, a Gold Glove fielder, and a tremendous power hitter.

- **Albert Belle**—Just look at the numbers. They are so huge, he just dominates year after year.

- **Mark McGwire**—Seventy home runs in one season. 'Nuff said.

- **Sammy Sosa**—Sixty-six home runs in one season. Ditto.

# *Five Games I Remember*

I have been playing baseball for quite a while and, in many ways, every game is memorable. But some certainly stand out. Here are five that stand out for me:

- Game 6 of the 1995 World Series against the Cleveland Indians. This was my best game as a pro. I threw a one-hitter and we won the World Series with that game. (See Chapter 4 for more.)

- Game 1 of the 1992 World Series against the Toronto Blue Jays. I had struggled in Game 6 of the National League Championship Series (NLCS) against Pittsburgh, and many fans were skeptical about the decision to start me in Game 1 of the World Series. But I pitched a complete game and we won 3-1.

- Game 7 of the 1992 NLCS against Pittsburgh. This is a game I was not involved in directly as a player. But I was there. It is the most exciting end to a ballgame I have ever been a part of. We were down 1-0 the whole game and Pittsburgh's pitcher, Doug Drabek, was just sticking it to us. In the ninth inning, we got a leadoff double and scored that runner. We had a runner on second, Sid Bream—one of the slowest runners in baseball. And Francisco Cabrera, who had spent 90 percent of the year in the minor leagues, came up to bat as a pinch hitter. On a two-strike, two-out pitch he hit the ball to left field, and we watched. There were so many things against us. Barry Bonds, the best left fielder in the game, was fielding the ball, and one of the slowest runners in baseball, Sid Bream, was trying to score. But it worked. Bream scored and we went to the World Series.

- On June 16, 1995, I threw the first shutout ever thrown at Coors Field, known as a hitter's park. It is hard to throw a shutout in that park, and it was very gratifying.

- An extra-inning state championship game in Massachusetts my junior year was also memorable. My team won the championship on a bunch of crazy plays. We had one play where the winning run scored but the runner didn't tag third base and we caught it. Baseball is a game of youth, and this game was a highlight of my youth. I especially remember the exhilaration.

# Wow! Home Runs and Strikeouts

CHAPTER THREE

**THINK OF EXPLOSIONS OF JOY**—100 mile-per-hour fastballs slamming into the superhero-powered bat of Mark McGwire or Sammy Sosa.

Or think of missing—and the ball slapping into the catcher's mitt.

Think of baseball and you think of power.

When most people think of trying to hit a baseball so far as to make the old men exclaim "Wow," they can't even imagine it. And then there are the other glamour guys—the pitchers with the fire to make superheroes look silly and who make you respond with disbelief to what you are seeing and even hearing. Wow.

Yet there it is, as magical a moment as a great rock and roll song. The great, majestic home run. The dynamic, dramatic strikeout. You listen, you watch—you just can't believe it.

# *Baseball Is a Game of Numbers and History*

In America, there are social security numbers and such. In baseball, there are also numbers—significant numbers.

There are a lot of insignificant numbers as well because baseball may just be the most analyzed of all human endeavors. If you want to know how a guy bats against left-handers in the middle innings of a rainy day game on the third Tuesday of the month in Milwaukee, most likely someone out there knows. Not all of those numbers born in the search for minutia are worthwhile, though.

But there are some significant numbers that are mostly agreed upon:

- Home Runs

- Strikeouts

- Batting Average

- On-Base Percentage

- RBIs

- Steals

- Pitchers' Wins and Losses

- Earned Run Average (ERA)

- Innings Pitched

- Saves

Those numbers count so much. Yet so does style-of-play. But that is hard to count. Baseball loves to count and there are standards for each of those

numbers, standards that depend on many different opinions. The standard isn't standard.

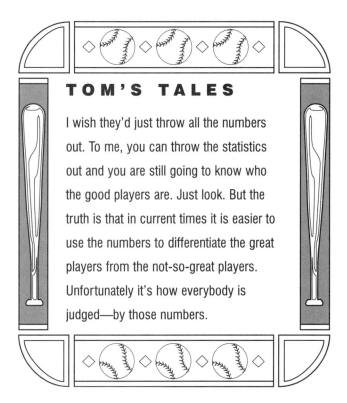

**TOM'S TALES**

I wish they'd just throw all the numbers out. To me, you can throw the statistics out and you are still going to know who the good players are. Just look. But the truth is that in current times it is easier to use the numbers to differentiate the great players from the not-so-great players. Unfortunately it's how everybody is judged—by those numbers.

Baseball, if anything, is a game of opinions. I'll take Mark McGwire and you take Willie Mays (or Mickey Mantle or Ted Williams or Reggie Jackson) and let's discuss it for a few hours. That's baseball—the best of all subjects. And there are numbers to back it up and ways to refute all numbers.

It helps people identify success and failure.

From a fan's standpoint, the numbers help identify the players who are successful. From a player's and manager's standpoint, the numbers are

scrutinized as they try to figure out what kind of a year a player is having—whether he is hot and can beat you at that given moment.

Numbers don't mean everything. But they are what they are and reputations for future generations only live in the record books. And, as we all saw in the summer of 1998, people pay attention.

## *Anybody Plays*

One of the appealing things about baseball is the fact that, even at the professional level, there is no size discrimination. You look at a baseball player and you think, *I can do that*. And you can. In one way or another, you can play baseball. Most Americans have played it, and many have played it competitively. The biggest player isn't always the best, and he may even be at a disadvantage. Baseball is the most representative sport—the big people and the not-so-big people all play.

**TIPS**

**TOM'S**

In baseball, heart, smarts, and savvy count as much as physical size. Heck, a guy my size can win the Cy Young Award—twice, with hopefully more to come. And I am not the only one. There are many, many great players who are normal-sized American men.

The game is for everyone. That's why the numbers count so much. In baseball, "more than anyone" means something.

# *The Great Home Run Hitters*

There it goes.

Again. And again. And, well, you get the picture. The home run is the $100 bill of baseball. There has been enormous interest in seeing a ball soaring over a major league fence since its invention, and Mark McGwire and Sammy Sosa took that interest and magnified it. If Mark or Sammy is batting, everybody wants to hear about it, including me.

If I am on the mound, it's a different story, but in general I am interested in what other players do, and nothing is more fascinating than what these two players do because they have made history. History happens all the time in baseball, but not like this. And yet in almost any ballpark at any given time in the summer, there is due up soon some Paul Bunyan of a man who can send the ball just as far—but not quite so many times.

Baseball has power hitters—men of glamour who are so large and intimidating as they walk to the plate that they can only be dealt with as predators. Pitchers tease them and challenge them, but everyone knows what could happen.

## THE 500 HOME RUN CLUB

Only 15 players have hit more than 500 home runs in their careers. These players are:

| | Player | HR |
|---|---|---|
| 1. | Hank Aaron | 755 |
| 2. | Babe Ruth | 714 |
| 3. | Willie Mays | 660 |
| 4. | Frank Robinson | 586 |
| 5. | Harmon Killebrew | 573 |
| 6. | Reggie Jackson | 563 |
| 7. | Mike Schmidt | 548 |
| 8. | Mickey Mantle | 536 |
| 9. | Jimmie Foxx | 534 |
| 10. | Willie McCovey | 521 |
| 11. | Ted Williams | 521 |
| 12. | Eddie Matthews | 512 |
| 13. | Ernie Banks | 512 |
| 14. | Mel Ott | 511 |
| 15. | Eddie Murray | 501 |

Pitchers know it. Fans know it. Fielders know it. Even the umpires. Everybody sees the big guy come to the plate and there are expectations. Maybe you don't expect a home run. But you do expect a moment, and rarely are you disappointed. Power hitters have a swagger.

## THE TEN BEST HOME RUN SEASONS

These are the 10 best seasons any player has ever had for hitting home runs:

| PLAYER | HOME RUNS | YEAR |
|---|---|---|
| 1. Mark McGwire | 70 | 1998 |
| 2. Sammy Sosa | 66 | 1998 |
| 3. Roger Maris | 61 | 1961 |
| 4. Babe Ruth | 60 | 1927 |
| 5. Babe Ruth | 59 | 1921 |
| 6. Jimmie Foxx | 58 | 1932 |
| 7. Hank Greenberg | 58 | 1938 |
| 8. Hack Wilson | 56 | 1930 |
| 9. Ralph Kiner | 54 | 1949 |
| 10. Babe Ruth | 54 | 1920 and 1928 |

Home runs require a certain amount of muscle, adrenaline, focus, and coordination. Home run hitters often succeed, and when they do, it is amazing.

# *Pitching to the Great Home Run Hitters*

*Not this guy.*

*There is no way I want this guy to beat me.* That's my attitude when I pitch to a power hitter, and the best example of such a player is Mark McGwire. If I am in an inning and I know Mark is due up, I am going to bear down extra hard on the guys before him. Although I know that any player in the major leagues is one of the 700 best in the world, some guys are more equal than others. It's just one of many ways that baseball is just like life. So I approach it that way.

When the big guy comes to the plate—and he will about four times a game—I want to do everything I possibly can to make sure the bases are empty. The worst possible situation is having to throw that player strikes. If, for instance, the bases are loaded, I cannot walk the power hitter. Inevitably, there is another good hitter next anyway. But I know that I cannot walk home a run.

I have to throw strikes to a power hitter—and he knows he's getting strikes. This is scary, because he can start to zone in.

Good luck to me.

# *Strikeout Kings*

First things first. I am not shy and I am proud of what I have accomplished. But I am not a strikeout king. I have whiffed a few guys in my time, and I plan on making another couple guys or so miss the ball before I am done, but I know I rely on other weapons. All pitchers have lots of weapons.

Some pitchers have cannons.

Some strike out 300 in a season by shooting arrows at upward of 95 mph and continuously daring hitters to take their shots. For instance, Roger Clemens has won five Cy Young Awards (and counting) by daring hitters to hit what they know is coming—precisely placed fastballs. And when he pitches, everyone watches.

| TOP TEN LEADERS IN STRIKEOUTS FOR A SEASON SINCE 1900 | | |
|---|---|---|
| 1. Nolan Ryan | 383 | 1973 |
| 2. Sandy Koufax | 382 | 1965 |
| 3. Nolan Ryan | 367 | 1974 |
| 4. Rube Waddell | 349 | 1904 |
| 5. Bob Feller | 348 | 1946 |
| 6. Nolan Ryan | 341 | 1977 |
| 7. Nolan Ryan | 329 | 1972 |
| 8. Nolan Ryan | 327 | 1976 |
| 9. Sam McDowell | 325 | 1965 |
| 10. Sandy Koufax | 317 | 1966 |

It is a thing of beauty—pure intimidation. It doesn't happen often. Usually, some kind of contact will be made. But from time to time, a power pitcher is so overpowering that he will face a batter and somehow create a situation in which any sane witness would have to testify under oath that the batter simply had no chance. Zero chance. *Here, go ahead. I dare you*, taunted the pitcher as he sent one of those blowtorch-fired baseballs past the confused batter. When it happens, the swing of a professional baseball player is nothing but the visual interpretation of a bad guess.

**T I P S**

**T O M ' S**

The key to hitting is timing, and the key to pitching is to upset timing.

The reason for the bad guess is not the cannon arm—or at least *not just* the cannon arm. There is always another weapon to keep the hitter off guard. If all a pitcher has is a fastball, even a great fastball, a major league hitter will figure it out. They have a gauge and within an at-bat or two, they can figure it out. It doesn't matter how fast it is. If a good hitter knows it is coming, he will figure it out. Strikeout kings make hitters look silly because they can make the hitter think about something besides the fastball. A good pitcher moves the ball around and makes a hitter think that *he could do anything*.

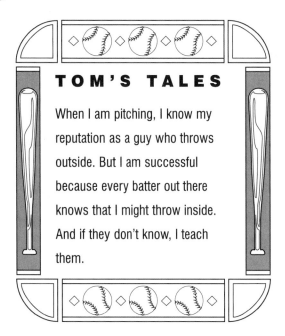

**TOM'S TALES**

When I am pitching, I know my reputation as a guy who throws outside. But I am successful because every batter out there knows that I might throw inside. And if they don't know, I teach them.

Then they heave it and the hitter either misses by a mile or else he is so frozen that he doesn't even swing.

# Batting Average

This is a simple number filled with a depth of meaning that most other numbers in baseball don't have. A hitter's batting average is like daily currency. It has value. When a batter has a good batting average, it means he gets on base a lot, and when he is on base he has a chance to score runs.

A batting average is calculated this way:

Total hits divided by total official at-bats.

It is not considered an official at-bat if a player walks, sacrifices, is hit by a pitch, or if there is an obstruction call on the catcher. But when a batter is safe because of an error, he does not get a hit, although it does count as an official at-bat.

So if you are hitting .380, that means you get on base 38 percent of the time, and you fail 62 percent of the time. And you are more than just great. You are a superstar. All hitters fail a lot. Batting average just shows who fails less.

# On-Base Percentage

This is a statistic that includes walks. What percentage of times does a hitter get on base? A player who has a good number in this category (anywhere in the high 40 percents) is not only a good hitter but also has a discerning eye. This is a crucial number.

On-base percentage is calculated this way:

Total hits + total walks + total times hit-by-pitch

Divided by

Total at-bats + total walks + total hit-by-pitch + total sacrifice flies

This number lets you know how often a player is really on base. This differs from batting average because it includes walks.

A walk is a weapon that should not be overlooked. That is why the on-base percentage is so telling. It gives a little more of the story than the batting average because a player who has a good eye and is able to get on

base is a great player to put up first. If the first batter on a team gets on base a lot it is a huge psychological weapon. If he is able to steal bases too, it's even better. Once a fast player is on base, he can cause havoc.

# RBIs

Runs Batted In (RBI) is a simple number that has tremendous meaning. Offense is all about runs. Players who knock in a lot of runs clearly produce when given an opportunity. Where they appear in the batting order is a place with lots of opportunities.

A batter earns an RBI from the official scorer if he drives a runner home with a hit, a sacrifice fly or a sacrifice bunt, a walk, a fielder's choice, or an error—if the official scorer rules the runner would have scored even if there wasn't an error. The batter will also be given an RBI if he is hit by a pitch and forces in a runner.

# Steals

Speed kills. It disrupts a pitcher's rhythm and it can even allow a team to score a run without the benefit of a hit. Speed on the base paths brings extra value to every foot that a ball travels when it is hit.

There have been teams, such as the St. Louis Cardinals of the 1980s, who could score a run without even getting a base hit. That same run would take other teams two hits to get. Single players are able to do that. Ricky

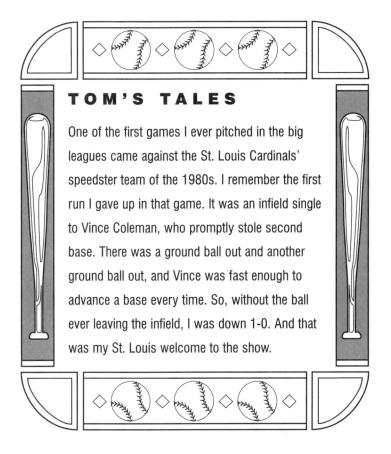

**TOM'S TALES**

One of the first games I ever pitched in the big leagues came against the St. Louis Cardinals' speedster team of the 1980s. I remember the first run I gave up in that game. It was an infield single to Vince Coleman, who promptly stole second base. There was a ground ball out and another ground ball out, and Vince was fast enough to advance a base every time. So, without the ball ever leaving the infield, I was down 1-0. And that was my St. Louis welcome to the show.

Henderson and Kenny Lofton come to mind. Occasionally, there are teams that can attack you.

When a player is on base, speed is a huge weapon. And it is not just the obvious reason of stealing bases and getting extra bases on hits. Speed distracts. When a pitcher is distracted, he often makes mistakes. And, coincidentally, most managers like to follow speed with power in the batting order. So, if a distracted pitcher who is worried about a fast runner makes a mistake pitching to a power hitter, what can happen? Can you say "Pow!"? Speed makes home runs happen. Speed kills.

## Pitcher's Wins and Losses

A pitcher gets a win if he starts a game, pitches for five innings, and is in the game when his team scores the run that eventually wins the game. If the pitcher is a relieving pitcher, not the starter, and he happens to be in the game when his team scores the run that eventually wins the game, he gets the win. A starter has to be in for five full innings to get the win. A reliever can get a win by throwing one pitch.

But what does a win mean? Well, wins are what it's all about, so a pitcher with a winning record is just about the most valuable commodity in all of baseball.

After all, the object of baseball is to win.

## Earned Run Average

Year to year, of course, there are some pitchers who are luckier than others. Some pitchers have more run support (in other words, their team scores more runs for them than others, therefore making it easier to win because he can give up more runs and still win).

Another good way to measure a pitcher is to look at his earned run average (ERA)—which tells, on average, how many earned runs he would give up in a nine-inning game.

An earned run is one that the other team "earns" with hits and walks. They are not runs that are the result of errors by the defense.

Earned Run Average is calculated this way:

Earned runs allowed (times nine) divided by innings pitched.

A pitcher's ERA shows how much of a chance he gives his team to win. If you are a pitcher, all you can realistically do is give your team a chance to win. You can't control the guy who's catching the ball behind you. You can't control how many runs your team scores. All that you can control is getting the other team out and not giving up many runs so that your team has a chance to win.

**TOM'S TIPS**

Three runs a game is a good average to have in the National League. Because the American League has a designated hitter (DH) hit for the pitcher, ERAs tend to be higher in the American League. But on average, if you give up three runs in the National League, your team will score three or four runs on most nights. So you have a chance to win.

## *Innings Pitched*

If a pitcher pitches a lot of innings, he is doing it because he is successful enough not to be pulled out. This ability gives his team a chance to win. Plus, every inning a starting pitcher pitches is one in which the bullpen gets to rest.

## Saves

A pitcher who can come in and finish off a close game has significant value. He is a weapon—looming in the sixth, seventh, and eighth innings as a ninth inning barrier. A good closer has a psychological affect on his team and on his opponent. If he is on a roll, both teams know it.

They know about it because he starts to accumulate saves. The best closers inevitably pitch for some of the best teams because they get the most chances. They come into a lot of games when their team is winning. All they have to do is get three outs.

A pitcher earns a save in certain circumstances: if he pitches during the final three innings of a game and his team wins; if he gets the final three outs in a game that his team is winning by three runs or less; if he gets the final out when he enters a game pitching to a batter who could score the run that ties the game.

## The Magic Numbers

In baseball, there are certain numbers that have a magic ring. For instance, from 1927 to 1961, the number *60* was the home run record held by Babe Ruth. In 1961, the magic number became *61* because Roger Maris hit that many home runs that year. Now, the magic number for home runs is *70*.

Here are a few other magic numbers from the world of baseball history, and what they mean.

70 — The most home runs hit in a season, set by Mark McGwire of the St. Louis Cardinals in 1998.

56 — The most games in a row that a player has gotten a hit in, set by Joe DiMaggio of the New York Yankees in 1941.

755 — The most home runs hit in a career by Hank Aaron.

511 — The most wins in a career, by Cy Young.

2,632 — The most games played in a row, set by Cal Ripken.

# The Modern Game

## CHAPTER FOUR

**THE CORE OF THE GAME WILL NEVER CHANGE:**

- The mound is 60 feet, 6 inches from home plate.

- The bases are 90 feet apart.

- There are 9 innings.

- If the weather doesn't take a turn for the worse, a team needs 27 outs to win.

Some things never change. Baseball is baseball, but some things have changed. Baseball is an ever-evolving sport and one of the most striking aspects of its evolution is the specialization of players. In the past, most teams used four starting pitchers and the same eight starting players every day. Now, most teams have five starting pitchers, a bullpen full of specialists, and a bench of role players who each bring a specific set of skills.

And in the 1990s, a key ingredient for the success of any team is financial stability. A team needs money to attract star players.

# *Before Curt Flood*

In 1969, as had happened thousands of times in baseball, there was a trade. The difference this time was that it involved Curt Flood. And Flood, who had a home in St. Louis, did not want to play for the Philadelphia Phillies, so he challenged baseball's reserve clause in court. This clause bound a player to his team, and the Supreme Court ruled that the clause was legal. But it was this challenge to baseball's established way that eventually led to the system of free agency that now exists. All players owe a debt of gratitude to the courage of Curt Flood.

Prior to 1969, baseball players had no freedom throughout their careers. Once you were on a team, you were the property of that team unless they traded you. Then you belonged to a different team. You had no leverage: You were paid what they decided you were worth.

Then Curt Flood challenged the reserve clause and, more than anything, he woke players up to the fact that they actually have rights. Curt Flood stood up and said, *I want to have a choice where I play*.

Suddenly, like a series of dominoes, events flowed forward for half a decade or so until the players and the owners agreed on a system that is still essentially in place. After six years of service, players not under contract are now allowed to negotiate with any team. They are free agents.

# The Unstoppable Force of Free Agency

Every year, it seems impossible to give more money to a baseball player and yet every year it happens. And, in many ways, the balance of power has suffered because of it.

There are many people who make a convincing argument that baseball has changed so that only certain teams are ever capable of winning. Their evidence is the disparity of payrolls—the best teams almost always have the highest payrolls. This disparity can be as much as $60 million—$80 million for one team and $20 million for another. Teams with low payrolls have a tough time competing.

**HOW IT HAPPENED**

Between 1949 and 1958, the New York Yankees won the American League Pennant eight of nine times. Only the Cleveland Indians won a pennant that year—by winning a record 111 games. (The record was broken in 1998 by the New York Yankees, who won 114 games.)

Baseball has eras of great teams, but today you can argue that teams are more fluid because players change teams more. Teams know that it takes money to lure good players. It's human nature. Think of any job. If you can make more money somewhere else you are certainly going to consider the economics. There are other considerations and I will delve further into a player's analysis of the market in Chapter 14.

Often one year after a player signs a huge contract, another player comes along with a bigger contract, making the first player seem, unbelievably, grossly underpaid.

I know.

Two years ago, I was a free agent and I signed my dream contract. Last year, I won the Cy Young Award for being the best pitcher in the National League, but I wasn't a free agent. Kevin Brown was, and now he makes almost twice as much as me for pitching in the National League. Timing is everything.

And next year, somebody else will probably make even more.

Despite it all, I know that a lot of players would like to do what I have done—stay with the same organization for their whole career. I am proud to have been with the Braves since I started. I may have taken a little less money to stay with the Braves than to totally test the free agent market. Although players often have reputations for chasing every last dollar, I think that there are many players who stay with their original team for less money than they may be offered elsewhere. It's a comfort factor. But remember that loyalty is a two-way street. Sometimes, the organization isn't loyal to the player. It's hard for a player to stay with an organization for a long time if he doesn't feel wanted. Of course, you also have to be good enough to stick around for a while to even have the choice.

# *The Character of the Game*

There are stories from the old days about players living in apartments around the corner from the ballpark and being part of the neighborhood. In the old days, guys got jobs in the winter.

In the old days people often knew the ballplayers, and although some players were celebrities, they were given room to be human. Now, players are paid enormous sums of money and are somehow accountable to the press or the public for almost everything they do—even off the field. I know that everything I do—good or bad—is potentially news.

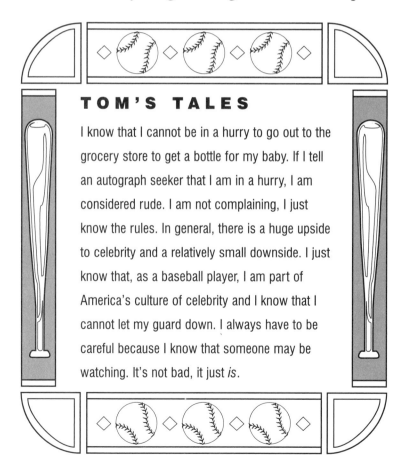

**TOM'S TALES**

I know that I cannot be in a hurry to go out to the grocery store to get a bottle for my baby. If I tell an autograph seeker that I am in a hurry, I am considered rude. I am not complaining, I just know the rules. In general, there is a huge upside to celebrity and a relatively small downside. I just know that, as a baseball player, I am part of America's culture of celebrity and I know that I cannot let my guard down. I always have to be careful because I know that someone may be watching. It's not bad, it just *is*.

Sure, we make more money. And we have nicer houses and we keep our-selves somewhat isolated. We have to because of the nature of the sport now. We are always on display. And, in the new culture of autograph seek-ing, we are always in demand.

# A Modern Milestone— Game 6 of the 1975 World Series

The greatest baseball game of all time was captured like a Norman Rockwell painting by television. In 1975, the Cincinnati Reds and my hometown Boston Red Sox met in a seven-game World Series won by the Reds. The series was epitomized by the dramatic sixth game.

To understand, you had to have waited for the rain to stop. For 72 hours in Boston, while the Cincinnati Reds held a 3 games to 2 lead over the Red Sox in the World Series, it rained.

And rained.

And rained.

And as Sparky Anderson's Big Red Machine of Johnny Bench, Joe Morgan, and Pete Rose waited, pitcher Luis Tiant of the Red Sox, who had won both Red Sox games in the Series, rested.

When the game finally began, Boston bolted to a 3-0 lead in the first inning on a Fred Lynn home run. Cincinnati tied the score in the fifth in-ning and sent Tiant to the showers in the eighth. At that point, Cincinnati was leading 6-3. They only needed six outs to win the World Series.

In the eighth inning, Pedro Bourbon, Cincinnati's fifth pitcher of the night, put two men on base and was relieved by Rawly Eastwick. Eastwick got two outs. The next batter due was Red Sox pitcher Roger Moret. But the Red Sox had a pinch hitter—Bernie Carbo, who proceeded to slam an Eastwick pitch into the center field bleachers. It was amazing. On the verge of absolute defeat, an unlikely pinch hitter propelled the Sox right back into it. Suddenly, this championship, earned after 162 games plus playoffs, had come down to sudden death. The Red Sox and Reds were tied after nine innings.

In the bottom of the twelfth, right-hander Pat Darcy was pitching for the Reds. The first batter of the inning was Boston catcher Carlton Fisk, who hit a cannon shot to left field. If it was fair, it was a home run. But if it was foul, the game would go on. Fisk jumped and waved and bounced down the line as he moved toward first base. Everyone in Fenway Park seemed to do the same. Collectively, a nation of baseball fans held their breath, and the ball went fair.

Carlton Fisk's dramatic twelfth inning home run to win Game 6 of the 1975 World Series epitomized the excitement of baseball in my youth.

AP / Wide World Photos

Although Fisk's home run was full of drama, this became a moment of Americana because of the way it was captured on television. The multitude of camera angles showing facial expressions and the joyous body language of a grown man leaping to the sky with happiness were enough to make this moment larger than life. When you saw it, you knew it was something special—dreams and hope and work, all tied with the hand of fate. In all the years of baseball, we had never seen anything like this before. We as viewers felt his joy. We saw what it must've been like to be Carlton Fisk on the day of his greatest athletic triumph. Television did that. Although the Reds went on to win the Series, this game lives on.

## *Camden Yards*

Next to an old warehouse in Baltimore, baseball entered a new era in 1992 when Oriole Park at Camden Yards opened. After a generation in which new ballparks seemed to have the same circular, cookie-cutter design, along came a revolutionary concept in the architecture of sports palaces— an attempt to make them look like the stadiums of old.

© MLB Photos

Baseball's new stadiums, such as Camden Yards in Baltimore, have tried to mix modern convenience with an old-time feel.

Camden Yards was the first such park in the major leagues, and its impact has been tremendous. Despite replacing the old Memorial Coliseum where the Baltimore powerhouses of old dominated, the new park brings a sense of astonishing history because of its design and placement in the middle of the city. By masterfully combining the old and the new, baseball finally figured out that its attributes should not be lost as time advances. Sure, things change, as some of the amenities of Camden Yards will attest. But Camden Yards, and other parks like it, are modern visions of an old style.

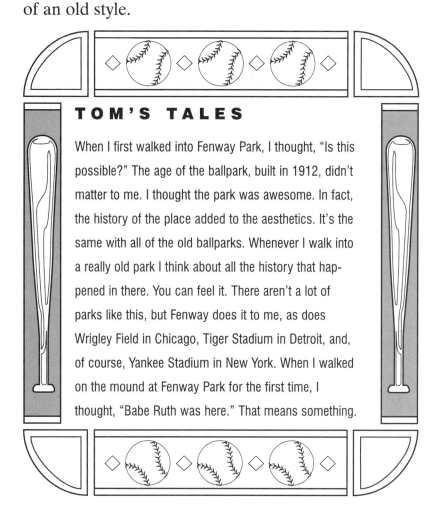

## TOM'S TALES

When I first walked into Fenway Park, I thought, "Is this possible?" The age of the ballpark, built in 1912, didn't matter to me. I thought the park was awesome. In fact, the history of the place added to the aesthetics. It's the same with all of the old ballparks. Whenever I walk into a really old park I think about all the history that happened in there. You can feel it. There aren't a lot of parks like this, but Fenway does it to me, as does Wrigley Field in Chicago, Tiger Stadium in Detroit, and, of course, Yankee Stadium in New York. When I walked on the mound at Fenway Park for the first time, I thought, "Babe Ruth was here." That means something.

The cookie-cutter ballparks served their purpose but I think they looked like what they were—the physical presence needed to portray baseball as a business. It wasn't like the old days when you went with your dad to the ballpark on a nice day and stayed as long as you could. It was different. These were parks that weren't just for baseball. They were simply there to serve a purpose, rather than to host a ballgame.

Certainly, a major reason for the construction of all of these new ballparks is the need for clubs to be able to come up with enough money to pay ballplayers. And so they do it by building new parks with lots of luxury boxes that attract corporate owners paying big bucks for the right to sit in a great seat with a group of friends or clients. These seats offer a number of things, including restaurant-style food service, television replays, and a great view. For me, when I go to see other sporting events such as a hockey game, I like sitting in them so I can actually watch the game instead of signing autographs for three periods. Of course, others sit in these seats simply because it is an enjoyable way to see a game—and they can afford it.

## The Strike of 1994

The World Series of 1994 was canceled.

It happened because the players and the owners couldn't agree on a fair way to split the incredible sum of money coming into the coffers of major league baseball. As an entertainment product, baseball is big *big* business and there is a lot to split. Just the same, there is more than one version of

the strike. I was the player representative of the Atlanta Braves. Here's my version:

It was about protecting free agency. The key idea for players is that there will only be a couple of times in your career, if you are lucky enough to have a long career, when you can choose where you work.

One of the first things that the owners wanted to do was to put in a salary cap, as there is in other sports. Essentially, a salary cap limits the amount of money that each team is allowed to spend—so that no one team can spend more than a set amount. Usually, a salary cap also has a low-end limit as well.

The owners didn't get the salary cap, but they did include a version of revenue sharing so that the five teams with the highest payrolls pay a sort of payroll tax to those teams with lower payrolls.

And when it comes to getting paid, baseball players know who is good. I can't say that I'm worth $8 million a year. Of course I'm

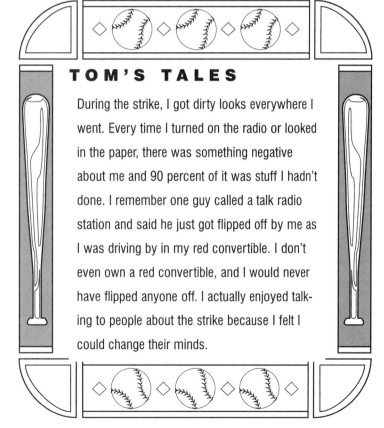

## TOM'S TALES

During the strike, I got dirty looks everywhere I went. Every time I turned on the radio or looked in the paper, there was something negative about me and 90 percent of it was stuff I hadn't done. I remember one guy called a talk radio station and said he just got flipped off by me as I was driving by in my red convertible. I don't even own a red convertible, and I would never have flipped anyone off. I actually enjoyed talking to people about the strike because I felt I could change their minds.

## HOW IT WORKS

In 1999, those five teams with the highest payrolls are scheduled to pay a 34 percent tax on the portion of their payrolls over a certain threshold. The threshold is the mid-level between the fifth highest payroll and sixth highest. In other words, all five teams above that threshold must pay a tax on all salaries that they pay that exceed the threshold. So, if the threshold is $60 million, and a team has an $80 million payroll, they must pay a tax on $20 million. This money goes to the five teams with the lowest local net revenues.

not, except that someone is willing to pay it to me. And I am not saying that I couldn't live happily ever after if I only made $5 million a year. Of course I could. But if there is another player at my position making $7.5 million and I am doing better year after year, I deserve to be paid equal or more. That's all.

In the end, though, the strike cost everyone money. The owners did win some concessions on a tax on teams with a high payroll, and the players maintained free agency.

The fans lost.

We all know that the fans lost. It hurts us to think that the game was damaged for a while after that summer. But baseball, as it always does, triumphed. Not even the horrible summer of 1994 could destroy the great game.

# *The 1995 World Series*

After the strike, for the first time in my life I dreaded going to the park and pitching. But I was also strong enough mentally to know that the only way I could move beyond the labor issues was to go out and have a good year. I did.

We did.

It was a great year for the Atlanta Braves. We came into the playoffs that year as a team that had been in the playoffs and the World Series but had not yet won it all.

In the first round, we faced Colorado with the first two games in Colorado. We were lucky enough to come out of there with two wins and then we won our final game at home. The next round for the National League Championship was against the Cincinnati Reds, and a lot of people predicted we would lose. But we had a great series and did everything right and we swept them in four games.

The match-up in the World Series was a perfect setup—the best offensive team in baseball—the bashing, mashing Cleveland Indians—against the Atlanta Braves—known for our pitching. These drastically different approaches met for six tense games.

In Game 6, when we were winning 3 games to 2, I pitched. This was an opportunity to give the Braves' organization a championship—something it had never gotten. We had come tantalizingly close twice before but both times we had swallowed a bitter pill. Game 6 to me was an opportunity. It was a chance to erase everything that had happened as far as the strike,

a chance to get the people who hated me on my side, and a chance to eliminate my childhood ghosts of cheering for the heartbreaking Boston Red Sox.

It was certainly a chance to be distracted.

I could have tried to do too much or to make too much out of that one game. But I was able to relax most of the day and not really think about it until an hour or so before it started. When I left the bullpen, I knew I had good stuff. But up until that year I had been notorious for having bad first innings, so I knew that my goal was to get out of the first inning unscathed. If I did that, I could go on from there. It was just a matter of batter to batter, inning to inning. So, that's how I approached it and that's how my opponent, the ultra-competitive Dennis Martinez, approached it. We battled: him against me, me against his lineup, him against mine.

And in the sixth inning Dennis Martinez was no longer in the game—but I was—when David Justice hit a shot off of Jim Poole. We went on to win the game 1-0. I pitched eight innings and got the win.

We won the World Series!

**There is nothing sweeter in all of sports than to win a championship.**

When the final out flew to our center fielder, Marquis Grissom, it all passed before me in slow motion, like a movie. I could see the whole strike, spring training, and the season. And then I felt the glory of a championship. I was honored to be named MVP of the Series.

I had won a championship before, a state championship in high school, but this was so much bigger. I was with a group of guys who had started out together losing 100 games a year in the 1980s, and now we were World Series champions. It just made it that much better.

# *The Magical 1998 Season*

The healing is complete.

All of the damage rendered by the strike of 1994 was repaired in the astonishing, record-breaking summer of 1998. First, there was the Mark McGwire and Sammy Sosa show. Wow. Breaking Roger Maris' thirty-seven-year-old record of sixty-one home runs in a season is astonishing enough. But it was not just broken; two *(two!)* people shattered it—in the same year! Mark hit seventy, Sammy hit sixty-six.

**Mark McGwire and Sammy Sosa captivated all the world with their heroics in 1998.**

David Wells threw a perfect game (no hits, no walks, no errors) for the New York Yankees, who, incidentally, won the most American League games in one season ever—114.

Cal Ripken, after playing in more games in row than anybody ever, decided to sit down. Wow.

The only thing that could've been better would have been a World Series between the teams with the two best records—the Yankees and Braves. But the Padres beat us fair and square, and the Yankees won the Series. All in all, it was an incredible season. Wow. Baseball as a modern game is back.

# How It Works

**BASEBALL IS THE PERFECT GAME.** One person throws a *ball*, another stands at *home plate* and tries to hit the ball with a *bat*. If he does, nine people try to catch it. Meanwhile, the person who hit the ball runs to *first base*—and, if there's time and opportunity—runs to *second base*, *third base*, and back to *home plate*. If he makes it around the bases and back to home plate during an *inning* without getting *out*, he scores one *run*.

Baseball is more complicated than that, so Part Two will tell you about the game itself and how it works.

# A Game of Symmetry

## CHAPTER FIVE

**BASEBALL IS A PERFECT GAME.** The poetry of baseball comes from the dimensions of the field and the symmetrical way each team attacks the other. I repeat these numbers from the last chapter because they are worth repeating:

• The mound is 60 feet, 6 inches from home plate.

• The bases are 90 feet apart.

• There are 9 innings.

• If the weather doesn't take a turn for the worse, a team needs 27 outs to win.

The great sportswriter Red Smith once wrote, "Ninety feet between bases is the nearest to perfection that man has yet achieved."

# *The Bases and the Pitcher's Mound—Perfect*

If the dimensions of the bases and the pitcher's mound were to change even a little, it would have an enormous impact on how the game is played. If, for instance, the mound were one foot closer to home plate, it would change the abilities of many players. For instance, I would suddenly be known as a power pitcher, and someone like Roger Clemens would be out of this world. On the other hand, if the mound were moved back one foot, Roger Clemens would probably be considered a finesse pitcher and I would be out of baseball.

### HOW IT HAPPENED

In 1968, Bob Gibson of the St. Louis Cardinals won the Earned Run Average (ERA) title in the National League with a ridiculously low 1.12 ERA. Many pitchers had astonishingly low ERAs that year and Carl Yastrzemski won the American League batting title with a low .301 average. Major league baseball responded by lowering the mound five inches.

One foot means one foot on a fastball. That's a lot. That's probably a few miles an hour on a fastball. You can do a lot more with a 91 mph fastball than one that is 87 mph. It's not much, but it is enough.

If the bases were 89 feet apart, or 91 feet apart, baseball wouldn't be the same.

# The Defense Starts with the Ball

In simple terms, a baseball game works this way:

• Each team has nine players.

• One team is "at bat" and the other team is "in the field."

The team in the field uses its nine players in these positions—and each has a corresponding number used in scoring.

| POSITION | CORRESPONDING NUMBER FOR SCORING |
|---|---|
| Pitcher | 1 |
| Catcher | 2 |
| First Baseman | 3 |
| Second Baseman | 4 |
| Third Baseman | 5 |
| Shortstop | 6 |
| Left Field | 7 |
| Center Field | 8 |
| Right Field | 9 |

© Chris Hamilton, Atlanta, GA

A baseball is 8.5 inches in circumference and weighs 4⅛ ounces without a cover. The cover is sewn by hand, and each has 108 stitches.

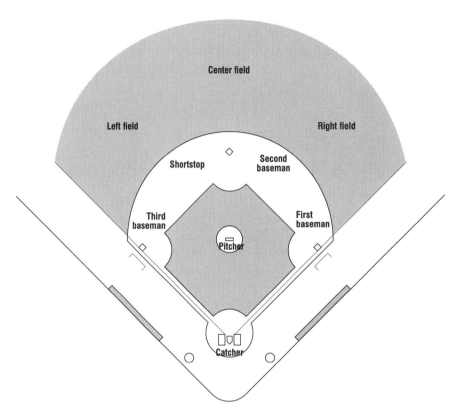

**This is where players typically play, although players often shift some depending on the abilities of the batter.**

Although the game is live at all times if there are base runners, it is played pitch by pitch when there are no runners on base. This is because a batter cannot normally do anything unless the ball is being pitched to him.

Occasionally, if a third strike is not caught by the catcher, the batter can run to first base. (More on this in chapter 6.) In all other cases, a batter can only wait for a pitch.

The pitcher throws the ball, therefore the pitcher controls the flow of the action.

# The Count

Pitchers throw either balls or strikes.

It takes four balls to walk a batter. If a batter walks, he goes to first base and becomes a *base runner* on first base.

It takes three strikes to strike out a batter. If a batter strikes out, he is out and his turn at bat is over until the other eight players in the batting order all get a chance to bat.

In between, there is a count—the number of balls and strikes. So, a 3-1 count means a batter has three balls and one strike. One more ball and he walks. Two more strikes and he strikes out.

Or he could hit the ball.

# What Happens to a Batter

The batter enters the area next to home plate—the area called the batter's box. The pitcher is on a mound, 60 feet, 6 inches from home plate, and he must keep his back foot on a rubber rectangle that is 24 inches long by 6 inches wide. He then goes into his windup (more in Chapter 17) and steps toward home plate, attempting to throw the ball over the plate and into a hittable zone between the top of the batter's knees and his armpits. If the ball travels in that trajectory, and it is not hit, it is a strike.

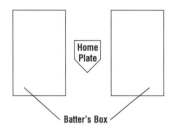

Home Plate

Batter's Box

Once the batter is in the batter's box, the pitcher is allowed to throw a pitch. If it travels over the plate between the top of the player's knees and his armpits, and he doesn't hit it, it is a strike.

If the pitch is not over the plate it is not a strike. It is a ball. If it is over the plate but above a line parallel with the player's armpits or below a line parallel with the top of the player's knees, it is not a strike. It is a ball—unless the batter swings at the ball and misses.

In all cases, when a batter swings and misses, it is a strike.

## HOW IT HAPPENED

In the 1870s batters could request a high pitch or a low pitch—belt to the shoulders, or belt to the knees.

If the batter swings and hits the ball but it does not travel between the white lines of the playing field, it is a foul ball. This counts as a strike if there are zero strikes or if there is one strike. If there are two strikes and the ball is fouled, the count does not change.

If the batter hits the ball in fair territory—between the white lines on the field—it is a fair ball. When there is a fair ball, the game gets interesting.

If the ball is hit in the air (even in foul territory outside of the white lines) and it is caught by the defense it is an out.

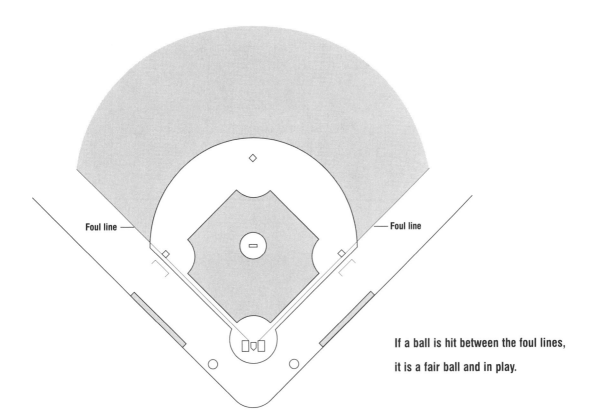

Foul line

Foul line

If a ball is hit between the foul lines, it is a fair ball and in play.

If the ball is hit in the air and it is not caught on a fly, the hitter can run to first base. The fielders can then throw the ball to the man covering first base—usually the first baseman—to try to get him out.

The same rule applies if the ball is hit on the ground. As soon as the batter hits the ball in fair territory, he can run to first base. The defense must then field the ball—a fly that is now bouncing, or a ground ball—and try to throw the runner out at first. A runner is out at first base if the ball is caught by a player covering the base (with any part of his body—usually his foot—on the base) before the batter touches the base. The runner is also out if he is actually "tagged" with the ball. If neither of these two things happen, he is safe—and allowed to stay on the base. The hand holding the ball (including if the ball is in a glove) must be the one that makes the tag on the body of a batter or runner.

### HOW IT WORKS

An "error" is called when the ball is hit or thrown to a fielder and the official scorer—a person in the press box—rules that the fielder should have caught the ball.

**WHAT IS IT?**

When there is not an error, generally,

- It is a single if the batter hits the ball and runs successfully to first base and stops.
- It is a double if the batter hits the ball and runs successfully to second base. A batter is automatically given a double if he hits the ball on a bounce over the outfield fence.
- It is a triple if the batter hits the ball and runs successfully to third base.
- It is a home run if the batter hits the ball and runs successfully around the bases to home plate. A batter automatically gets a home run if he hits the ball on a fly over the outfield fence.

# *Outs and Innings*

The game is divided into nine innings.

Each team is allowed three outs per inning. I already explained the basics of how an out occurs. The team's turn at-bat is finished if they have three outs; then they must take the field and give the other team a turn to bat.

When both teams have had a turn at-bat and have three outs, an inning has been played. The game ends after nine innings, unless the score is tied.

**HOW IT WORKS**

The home team always bats last in every inning. If the home team is winning after the visiting team has finished batting in the ninth inning, the game is over. After all, they are already winning, so it is logical. Why keep playing since the other team can't bat again anyway?

So how do you score?

Well, remember there are three bases—first, second, and third—plus home plate. A player who first comes to bat must run to each base in order without being tagged out, and he scores "a run" when he touches home plate. If at any time he is tagged while not on a base, he is out.

The team with the most runs at the end of the game wins.

## Umpires' Signals

The folks in charge of a baseball game are called umpires. They enforce the rules.

First, they "call" balls and strikes. That's right, their job is to interpret the pitch.

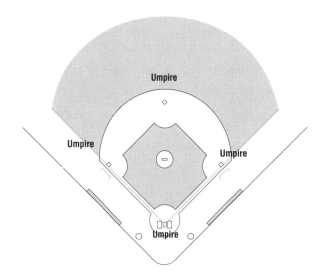

When there are no runners on base, this is the standard positioning of the four umpires. As runners appear on base, umpires shift in subtle ways to see the play better and to be in a position that won't interfere with play. In the playoffs and World Series, two extra umpires are added for each game. These umpires play along the lines in the outfield, judging fair and foul balls and making calls on whether balls were caught.

### HOW IT WORKS

Remember that umpires always have individual variations that coincide with the official style of how to call a play. They make the calls the right way, yet they all do it differently.

Players are not allowed to argue with umpires about whether a call is a ball or a strike. If they were, there would be arguments all day long because many pitches in a major league game are right on the border between a ball and a strike. Every hitter thinks the pitch is a ball and every pitcher thinks the pitch is a strike.

© Chris Hamilton, Atlanta, GA

When there is a ball, the umpire yells "Ball!" and he does not raise his arm. When there is a strike, he yells "Strike!" and he raises his right hand. Some umpires are more theatrical than others. Players always want an umpire to be definitive and quick with his calls.

**An umpire can call a strike in any number of theatrical ways— but his job is to make his decision clear.**

On plays in the baselines, they also call out and safe. When he calls safe, he extends his arms like this:

© Chris Hamilton, Atlanta, GA

**When an umpire calls safe, it means the runner can stay at the base, or it means that a run has been scored across home plate.**

When a runner is out, an umpire yells "Out!" while throwing his arm out and around like this:

© Chris Hamilton, Atlanta, GA

**An umpire is always clear so a runner knows when he is out.**

If a batter checks his swing and the home plate umpire calls a ball, the catcher can ask for the call to be appealed to an umpire on a corner base. The appeal for a right-handed batter would go to the first base umpire, and the appeal for a left-handed batter would go to the third base umpire.

The appeal questions whether the barrel of the bat crossed over home plate before the batter pulled it back. Since the umpire down the line has a direct view of the barrel of the bat, he makes the final judgment in questionable swings. An appeal is made by the catcher.

If the base umpire thinks the player swung (in other words, if he thinks the barrel of the bat crossed over home plate before it was pulled back) he raises his arm to indicate a strike call. If the umpire thinks the player did not swing, the umpire just stands there.

Umpires also make the call if a ball is hit fair or foul. As soon as an umpire knows, he simply raises both arms above his head and waves in the direction that the ball fell.

They call for the Infield Fly Rule and they call balks (more in Chapter 7). In both cases, they stop the action and yell the call.

## *Run in a Circle Back to Home*

When a batter hits the ball, he runs to first base. If he is safe on first base, he wants to continue around the bases to second, third, and finally all the way back to where he started—home plate. If a runner makes it around the bases without getting tagged out, and without his team making three outs, he scores a run.

He scores as soon as he touches home plate safely.

So, if he hits the ball and is safe at first, he can keep running to second base on his hit, but he risks getting tagged out. If he decides to stay at first base, he can wait for the next batter or try to steal second base. If he tries to run, the other team can tag him out.

If he waits for the batter, he can get to second base in a number of ways:

- If the batter walks, the runner automatically is awarded second base.

- If the batter hits the ball and no one catches it, he runs to first base, so the runner that was on first base must run to second base.

- If the batter hits the ball on the ground and the runner runs to second without getting tagged out or forced out, he is safe. Since the batter is running to first, the runner is "forced" to go to second base. Therefore, the defense doesn't have to tag the runner to get him out. It can also tag second base. Or it can try to throw the runner out at first.

- If the batter hits a fly ball that is caught, the runner cannot leave his base until the ball is caught. The fielder who caught the ball must throw it to a teammate who can tag the runner before he reaches second base. If the player reaches second base first, he is safe.

- If the batter hits the ball on the ground and is thrown out at first, the runner on first base can run to second base. This is called "a sacrifice" by the batter.

Once the runner is on second base, the strategy works the same way, except that he really is allowed to keep running as long as he wants. If he thinks he can get to the next base—as long as there is no time-out called by the umpire—he can run. Of course, the defense can try to throw him out.

But the idea of a batter in baseball is to go from:

Home Plate
> ➤To First Base
>> ➤To Second Base
>>> ➤To Third Base
>>>> ➤Back To Home Plate

No other sport is like baseball. In almost every other team sport, you start on one end and you try to get to the other end and score. In baseball, you start where you want to end up—home plate. If you don't get to where you already are, then you haven't accomplished anything.


# *Different Fields*

Although the distance between the bases—90 feet—and the distance between home plate and the pitcher's mound—60 feet, 6 inches—is constant, it is also true that there are many different kinds of fields.

• Some teams play indoors, in domes on artificial turf.

• Some teams play outdoors on grass.

• Some teams play outdoors on artificial turf.

• Some teams play in retractable domes that can make an outdoor game into an indoor one in about 20 minutes, and vice versa.

• Some teams have smoothly curving outfield walls that are the same height across the outfield.

• Some teams have an outfield fence with jigs and jags or different heights in different parts of the outfield. The wall in left field at Fenway Park, for instance, is 35 feet tall. It is aptly named The Green Monster.

When you have a special kind of field, such as Fenway Park with its short left field wall that is nevertheless tall, you want to attract players for that configuration. For instance, Boston teams have traditionally been built with power hitters who can loft flies over that wall, or who can pound high line drives off of it for easy doubles.

Not a lot of parks have a special character that influences how its team is chosen. Here are three:

• Fenway Park in Boston—It's a small stadium to cover defensively so you can sacrifice some speed in the outfield for power in the bats. Most Red Sox teams for the past eighty years have done just that.

• Busch Stadium in St. Louis—This is a big ballpark with artificial turf. It has a faster surface and a big outfield so the Cardinals have often been a team with a speedy outfield that relies on speedsters on offense as well as defense.

• Yankee Stadium in New York—This park has a devastatingly short right field fence, which favors a good left-handed power hitter. The Yankees have had a few, including one named Babe Ruth.

The problem with building a team for your ballpark is that even though you get to play 81 games in your park, you also have to play 81 games in other stadiums. You need a bit of a mix, but no one will ever argue that you shouldn't take advantage of playing 81 games in one place.

# *No Clock*

Baseball is not like other end-to-end games that find their drama in the cruel reality of a ticking clock. Baseball does what it wants, when it wants. You never really know when a baseball game will end.

In other sports, there is a concept of "killing the clock" in which the team with the ball (or puck, or whatever object they chase) is held by one team so that the other team cannot even try to score in the time remaining.

In baseball, teams take turns no matter what. As long as the game is still going on, the team that is losing has a chance to win. If your team is winning and the other team starts to rally, the last inning of a game can take a horrifically long time. If your team is rallying and you win, it all happens too fast.

Baseball is the only game that allows for last-minute comebacks of monumental proportions. That's because in baseball, there is no last minute. There is only a last chance.

# The Positions and the Designated Hitter

CHAPTER SIX

**BASEBALL PLAYERS HAVE JOBS AND WEAR UNIFORMS.** They play baseball as businessmen play at business, filling specific roles with a variety of responsibilities.

On defense, baseball is a game of real estate: one baseball, one batter, and nine players on defense covering the field. The jobs, although limited by the rules and how the game is played, are really quite flexible depending on who is at bat. In other words, you could put seven of those nine guys anywhere—if you wanted. The pitcher stays at the mound and the catcher stays at home plate, but the other seven players can and do move around.

Four infielders and three outfielders cover as much of the field as possible. More balls are hit to the infield, so more players are there to cover it. Since it takes the ball longer to get to the outfield, fewer men can and do cover more ground.

On offense, all players bat—however, in the American League the pitcher does not bat. In the American League, another player in the batting order—the designated hitter (DH)—bats for the pitcher and does not play the field; his job is to hit.

## What They Wear

The standard baseball uniform includes a jersey, pants, hat, and stirrups issued by the team; each player chooses his own shoes and fielding glove. Most players wear shoes with metal spikes on the bottom for traction, but in recent years some players have experimented with wearing sneakers.

**T I P S**

**T O M ' S**

For safety reasons, all major league ballplayers wear a jockstrap and a protective cup. All male ballplayers should.

Infielders (except for first basemen) tend to use a smaller glove than out-fielders. This is because they need to make a quick ball transfer in order to throw it. First basemen wear an extended glove with a pocket that can dig wide and errant throws from the dirt. A catcher wears a special padded glove that is designed to absorb the sting when catching a fastball.

All batters wear batting helmets to protect their heads.

**HOW IT HAPPENED**

The batting helmet didn't become mandatory until 1971.

Of all the players in the field, catchers wear the most equipment because they are in the most precarious position—behind the batter. Almost by definition, they take a beating. They wear a chest protector, shin guards, a protective helmet, a face mask (many catchers now wear a one-piece face mask and protective helmet that looks like a hockey goalie's mask), and a neck protector.

**Catchers are in constant danger of tipped and errant balls, so they wear lots of equipment to keep safe.**

© Chris Hamilton, Atlanta, GA

# *Nine Players on Defense—Divided by Two*

There is an infield, and there is an outfield. Infielders play in the infield, and outfielders play in the outfield. Both cover a specific "area," but they catch what they can get to. If two players are converging on a ball, one will yell "I got it!" or "Mine!" or something like that, and the other will back away. Communication is imperative in the field.

It is most important to be strong up the middle by having two strong middle infielders—the second baseman and the shortstop. The center fielder and the catcher are also up the middle. Middle infielders are the most important defensive positions because they generally have a chance to catch more balls.

# *Infield*

Infielders are the most important players. Their primary job is to catch ground balls and throw the ball accurately to first base. The first baseman's job is to catch balls thrown to him by other infielders.

Picking up a ground ball is more complicated than it looks. The ball could do almost anything. If, for instance, you are on astroturf, the ball is going to skip a bit and pick up speed as it first shoots through the infield. On natural grass, the ball tends to slow down a bit as it bounces, but there are more variables—the ball hits a rock or even a footprint and changes direction, even a little.

**T I P S**

**TOM'S**

A field that has a bad infield is something that affects all players. Some know it better than others do. If you watch on television, major league baseball players make it look easy, but the truth is that it is not easy. Players make it look easy because they have practiced thousands and thousands of times. And, some players make it look easier because they know the field as their home field. It *does* make a difference.

Infielders try their best to know the field, but they always know their role in their position:

**FIRST BASE:** The first baseman handles almost all throws to first base after a ground ball. He handles all ground balls hit his way. He covers the base when there is a runner on base. The first baseman comes in when there is a bunt to his side of the infield. First basemen are expected to hit for average and power.

**SECOND BASE:** The second baseman handles all ground balls hit his way and turns the pivot on double play balls hit to the third base side of the infield. He often covers throws to second base—either from the catcher on steals or from the pitcher on pick-off plays. He gets all cutoff throws from right field. Second basemen are expected to hit for average; power is an extra at this position.

The second baseman and shortstop spend time around second base as they catch the ball, tag the base, and then throw it on to first base. All the while, they must avoid a runner who is barreling toward them.

© Chris Hamilton, Atlanta, GA

**SHORTSTOP:** The shortstop is the captain of the infield. When defensive plays are called about who covers the bag on certain plays, it is the shortstop who gives the signal by covering his mouth with his glove so that only his teammates can see a signal—usually an open mouth or a closed mouth signifies one of two options. Over the course of a year, shortstops probably get the ball hit to them more than any other position. It is the one position in baseball that sacrifices some offense for spectacular defense. Defense at this position is necessary. A shortstop covers all ground balls hit his way, and he pivots on double play ground balls hit to the first base side of the infield. He gets all cutoff throws from left field. Shortstops of the modern era are getting bigger and some are hitting for spectacular average and power. But generally, shortstops are known for defense and any offense at all is a bonus.

**THIRD BASE:** The third baseman covers what is called "the hot corner" because many hot shots come off the bats of big right-handed power hitters and they fly right at third base. You have to be on your toes over there or you can get killed. Third base is a reactive position. There isn't a lot of time to think. Many players who struggle at shortstop early in their career find a home at third base. Third basemen cover ground balls that come their way and they cover all plays at third base. They have to be adept at making tags because many plays at third are tag plays. And they must have a strong, accurate arm to make the throw to first base. They also cover bunts hit to their side of the infield. Third basemen are expected to hit for average and power.

# *Outfield*

Outfielders catch long fly balls. They also hopefully cut off any balls hit in gaps (gaps are areas between fielders) and throw the ball into the infield in time to stop a runner from going for an extra base. And if the ball is hit off the outfield fence, they catch it on a bounce as it ricochets off.

Communication is a key skill of outfielders because they need to know when to go for the ball and when to back up. Over time, with good outfielders, it develops beyond just yelling, "I got it!" You can actually see players begin to work together. Automatically, one goes for the ball and the other goes behind. The general rule is that the center fielder goes for everything he can get to and the other outfielders back him up.

Although the outfield positions are similar, each plays a different role:

**CENTER FIELDER:** The center fielder is the captain of the outfield. He catches everything he can reach. If he calls for the ball, the other players get out of the way. The center fielder is generally a fast player because he has a lot of ground to cover. Of all the outfielders, he is the one who shifts the most, batter to batter. Generally, at bat a center fielder is a speedy player who hits for average and is a menace on the base paths.

**RIGHT FIELDER:** The right fielder is generally the outfielder with the strongest arm because the throw from right field to third base is the longest throw in a baseball game. One key to picking a right fielder is the skill of your center fielder. If a team has a great center fielder who can get lots of balls, it can get away with an adequate right fielder as long as that player can hit for power. This is an exciting position to watch because the ball comes off the bat with a weird spin to right field. Right fielders need to learn to interpret the spin off the bat.

**LEFT FIELDER:** The left fielder doesn't always have to be the most talented player because the ball is usually true when it is hit to left field. In other words, there aren't many weird spins except for those off of left-handed batters, and there are fewer left-handed batters than right-handed batters. A left fielder can get away with having an average arm because the throw into third from left field is not nearly as far as the throw from right field. Left fielders, like right fielders, are expected to be power hitters.

# *Pitchers on Defense*

Pitchers throw the ball. But they do a lot more than that.

Beyond the art of pitching, pitchers must keep base runners on base and they must help the catcher throw out base runners by getting the pitch into home quickly. They must catch balls hit their way and cover bunts in front of home plate. Almost anytime a ball is in play, the pitcher has to be somewhere backing up a potential throw—anticipating where the ball is going and where the play might be.

**TOM'S TIPS**

All players, before every pitch, think to themselves: *How many runners are on base? How many outs are there? If the ball is hit to me, what am I going to do with it?* Before it is ever hit to them, they already know what to do because there isn't time to think about it when the ball is in their glove. At that point, it's time to do something, not just think about doing something.

Pitchers back up different plays based on the number of outs and whether there are runners on base. You have to know where the logical play would be and then back up that potential throw, lining up behind a line from the ball to the potential receiver of the throw. In other words, pitchers simply back up a throw in case it is missed.

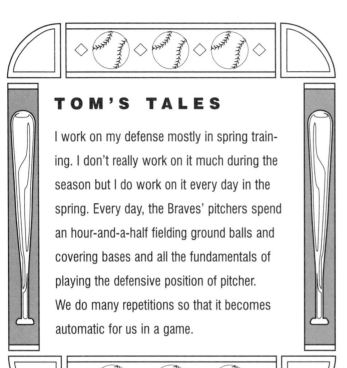

**TOM'S TALES**

I work on my defense mostly in spring training. I don't really work on it much during the season but I do work on it every day in the spring. Every day, the Braves' pitchers spend an hour-and-a-half fielding ground balls and covering bases and all the fundamentals of playing the defensive position of pitcher. We do many repetitions so that it becomes automatic for us in a game.

Pitchers, like all players, play a crucial role in defense. I am a big believer that the defensive role of a pitcher is very important. If a pitcher is known as a good pitcher but is a defensive liability, it could mean a number of things: he is weak on the fundamentals of backing up; he isn't a good fielder; he doesn't hold runners on base well; he doesn't throw well after he catches the ball. In any case, he hurts his cause the same as any bad fielder would hurt his cause.

A pitcher is one of the nine players. A pitcher is an infielder. If the ball comes to me, as a pitcher, I try to catch it and throw the batter out. If I can get to the ball, I want it in my hands, not anyone else's.

# *Catchers*

Catchers catch pitches, but they do much more than that. A catcher puts a pitcher in a rhythm. If a catcher knows what a pitcher likes to do and how he likes to work in certain situations, it can help put a pitcher's mind at ease. Pitchers don't like to shake off four or five signs before getting a pitch that they want. Catchers able to get in synch with a pitcher are very valuable defensively.

It is most important for a catcher to call a good game. If he gives the team some offense, that is a bonus. Although the catcher is only making suggestions when he calls a pitch, it can be frustrating for a pitcher to work with a catcher who doesn't understand what is called for in different game situations.

Catchers cover bunts in front of home plate, and they cover home plate for most plays. Generally, they run and back up first base on infield ground balls. If a catcher can hit, it is great, but he is there for his defense and his ability to help a pitching staff.

# *Designated Hitter*

Look at almost any little league team and you will see that the best hitter on the team is generally the pitcher. Yet, in half of the major leagues—the American League—the pitcher doesn't even bat. And in the National League, where the pitcher does bat, most don't exactly rip up the ball.

I like batting. It helps keep me more involved in the game.

© Chris Hamilton, Atlanta, GA

Here's what happens, because it happened to me. I didn't hit at all for two years in the minor leagues. That's two years away from seeing 90 mph fastballs. Pitchers generally work on pitching, not hitting. So even though most pitchers were star hitters of their high school teams, they stop practicing. By the time they have spent four or five years in the minors developing their pitching skills, their batting skills have significantly eroded. The truth is that most major league pitchers are lousy hitters.

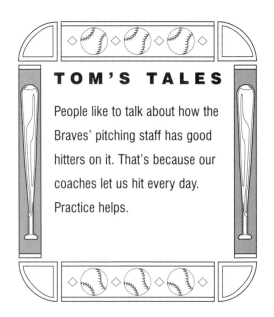

**TOM'S TALES**

People like to talk about how the Braves' pitching staff has good hitters on it. That's because our coaches let us hit every day. Practice helps.

And so in the American League and in many minor leagues associated with the American League, pitchers don't bat. Instead, there is a designated hitter (DH) who bats in place of the pitcher but does not play the field.

Generally, a DH is a big, lumbering home run-type hitter who isn't a great defensive player but is a big threat at the plate. Team ERAs in the American League are about a half a run higher because, for one reason, pitchers face that one extra good hitter. A DH is exactly that, a hitter. He is expected to be a run producer.

# The Infield Fly Rule and More

 CHAPTER SEVEN

**IT CAN BE A WEIRD GAME.**

If your relative from Antarctica visits and sees a fly ball hit into the infield with runners on first and second base and less than two outs, what in the world are they going to think when the umpire yells, "Out!" before anyone even catches the ball? What? Or what if the pitcher makes some odd little motion causing the umpire to yell "Balk!" and let the runner advance one base? Explain that to your cousin.

Even if you know the basics of baseball, there are essential quirks to understand in order to really *get* baseball. They all seem weird at first. But if you think about any of these rules, you understand that they are perfectly fair and marvel that someone actually suggested such an oddly right thing in a moment of clarity.

And if you really want to understand the game, you need to see that there is a dynamic in the interaction of umpires and players. All calls made by umpires are open to interpretation by players and fans, but once a decision has been made on the field it is in the books forever.

## The Infield Fly Rule

This is a rule that stops the defense from intentionally dropping the ball and getting three outs instead of one.

The rule is simply this: if there are men on first and second base and the ball is popped up into an area that is deemed by the umpire to be in the infield, the umpire yells "Infield Fly!" This means the batter is out, because if the rule didn't exist, the two runners on base would have two choices—to run or stay. If they ran, the fielder could catch the ball and activate the double play—both runners tagged out on base. If they stayed on base, the fielder could intentionally not catch the ball, throw it to one base and then have it thrown to the other base, forcing both runners out. It's just not fair. So baseball invented the infield fly rule to make sure that a fly ball in the infield results in one fair out, not two unfair outs.

## Strikeout, Safe at First

When there is a third strike, the catcher must catch the ball to record the strikeout. If he does not, the batter can run to first base. He must be thrown out or tagged out just as if he had hit the ball. If the batter makes it to first base safe, he is allowed to stay. This is called a strikeout with

either an error by the catcher or a wild pitch by the pitcher. If, for instance, a pitcher throws a curveball in the dirt, the batter swings at it and misses, and the catcher misses, it could be called a wild pitch. Most other instances of this play would be called an error by the catcher—also called a passed ball.

## Catcher's Interference

If the batter swings and his bat hits the catcher's glove, he is given first base. This sometimes happens because most catchers have a certain spot that they set up in, and from time to time a batter will stand far back in the batter's box and the catcher won't notice. Catcher's interference also occurs when a pitcher has crossed him up so that he is expecting a fastball and the pitch is a change-up. In this case, the catcher's glove is too far forward so the batter hits it.

## Runners Running Past Other Runners

If you are a base runner, you have to stay in your place. When a runner passes another runner, the runner who ran too far is out. This actually happens from time to time in the major leagues.

If, for instance, there is a runner on first base and the batter hits the ball into a gap, he runs as hard as he can to first base. But in that case the base runner waits between first and second to see if the ball will be caught. Sometimes, the batter, who is hustling but not looking, runs right past the runner. In this case the batter is out.

## The Balk

If a pitcher does something that is interpreted as an attempt to deceive the runner, it is a balk. If a balk is called, the runner on base is allowed to advance a base. If that scores a run, so be it. This is a rule.

© Chris Hamilton, Atlanta, GA

The Set Position is when a pitcher must stand completely without motion except for his head. A pitcher, once he is on the mound, can move his hands to a stopped—set—position. Then he cannot move anything but his head, unless he starts a pitch or a move to pick off a runner. Even a twitch will result in a balk call.

The simplest of all balks occurs when a pitcher starts his delivery toward home and then stops.

Then it gets more complicated.

It often depends on the foot that you use to stride. If you pull that foot behind the rubber, you must then throw to the plate. If you don't, it is a balk. Of course, the runner knows this too, so if he sees your striding foot cross that imaginary line, he can take off because he knows you are throwing home. You can't throw to first base at that point to attempt a pick-off. That would be a balk.

The balk rule gives the runner an advantage. Keeping a fast runner on base while still trying to pitch a ballgame is a game of cat and mouse.

**T O M ' S    T I P S**

To win the game of cat and mouse, I use the slide step. Instead of lifting my knee as I do in a normal windup, I simply lift my spikes out of the ground and then slide my stride toward the batter. Some pitchers say they lose power by using the slide step, but I find it works fine. I just have to work a bit harder on the push off because there is not as much momentum to carry the body.

Pitchers often try to deceive runners, and not everything they do is legal, but some things are. If you are on the mound, you can actually fake a throw to second base or to third base and it is not a balk.

Some umpires enforce the rules more strictly than others, and over time all players learn who is who. Some umpires call balks more often, so pitchers tend to be careful, especially once caught.

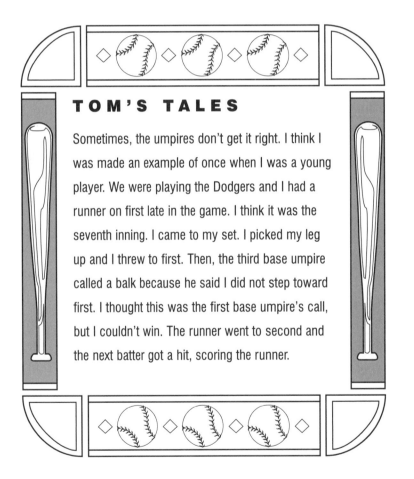

## TOM'S TALES

Sometimes, the umpires don't get it right. I think I was made an example of once when I was a young player. We were playing the Dodgers and I had a runner on first late in the game. I think it was the seventh inning. I came to my set. I picked my leg up and I threw to first. Then, the third base umpire called a balk because he said I did not step toward first. I thought this was the first base umpire's call, but I couldn't win. The runner went to second and the next batter got a hit, scoring the runner.

# *Umpires Are Human*

Players and managers have been arguing with umpires since the first baseball game. So many calls are close that the umpire is bound to make decisions that offend half the people in the game. That's baseball. And sometimes umpires are wrong. The good ones admit when they make a mistake. I think it is a classy thing to do and it shows that they are trying just as hard at their profession as we are at ours.

**T I P S**

**T O M ' S**

Umpires have to be psychologically tough. Every time they decide yes or no, an argument could ensue in which they appear to plead their case to the 50,000 people in the stadium and the millions more watching on television. Umpires have thick skins by design.

I believe that part of the charm of baseball is that it requires humans to make split-second decisions. I am not in favor of the instant replay. It would most likely take too long and take away from the flow of the game. The human element is what makes it baseball. It is a perfect game played and judged by imperfect humans. Well, umpires are right 99 percent of the time. And people talk about it forever.

# *Getting Tossed*

Once in a while, a player or manager will get tossed out of the game. Different players and managers react in different ways.

One of the more interesting instances happened a couple of years ago when our pitcher John Smoltz, one of the most mild-mannered players in baseball, got thrown out. At the time, John was pitching and there was a play at third base. It was a bang-bang kind of play where everything happened quickly. The guy slid in and somehow his hand came off the bag, and John was in a position to see it all. Actually, John was between the umpire and third base. The player was actually out but the umpire called him safe. John jumped as if to say "Come on!" As it happened, the umpire stepped on him but the umpire interpreted it as the other way around—as if John had stepped on the umpire. So just like that, John got thrown out of the game. It was interesting because mild-mannered John got thrown out. It just goes to show it can happen to anybody in the heat of a game.

Although it is only a game, some arguments with umpires can become heated.

© Chris Hamilton, Atlanta, GA

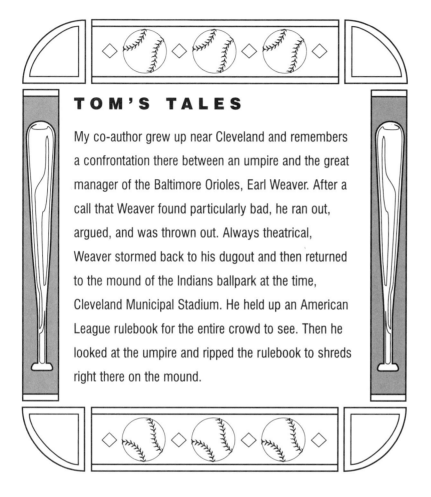

**TOM'S TALES**

My co-author grew up near Cleveland and remembers a confrontation there between an umpire and the great manager of the Baltimore Orioles, Earl Weaver. After a call that Weaver found particularly bad, he ran out, argued, and was thrown out. Always theatrical, Weaver stormed back to his dugout and then returned to the mound of the Indians ballpark at the time, Cleveland Municipal Stadium. He held up an American League rulebook for the entire crowd to see. Then he looked at the umpire and ripped the rulebook to shreds right there on the mound.

It happened to me once. It was horrible. I was thrown out for throwing at a batter. And I was guilty. It was horrible but it was just one of those baseball situations.

Early in my career in Atlanta I was pitching in the second part of a back-to-back series (meaning a set of games played in one town are followed by a set of games between the same two teams in the other city) with Philadelphia. In the game, our center fielder Otis Nixon got hit twice.

So when I pitched the next inning, I was supposed to follow the payback rules of baseball and throw at their leadoff hitter. Their leadoff hitter just happened to be Dale Murphy, a long-time icon and hero in Atlanta who was finishing out his career in Philadelphia.

Not only was Murphy an Atlanta hero, but he was a personal mentor to me when I first joined the Braves. He helped me out and he is a super nice guy. And I had to throw at him. So the first pitch I threw was about 70 mph and he just backed out of the way. The next pitch was the same and the same thing happened. Then the umpire said, "All right, if you do that again, you're out." I did it again, and by the time the pitch got to the catcher, he was out of the way. I received letters telling me I was a jerk for two years after that happened. And I never wanted to throw at him.

# The Players and Their Skills

PART THREE

**EVERYBODY HAS A JOB IN A BASEBALL GAME.** Responsibilities vary, yet all good baseball players have mastered certain fundamental skills.

In Part Three, I discuss the specific roles of each position on the field, and then I describe their fundamental skills.

# Four Infielders and Their Bats

CHAPTER EIGHT

**MOST PLAYS HAPPEN IN THE INFIELD.**

When the ball bounces on the dirt and grass (or artificial turf) infield, it is supposed to be good for the defense because infielders should catch ground balls and turn them into easy throw-to-first base outs.

Yet infielders do more than catch ground balls. They throw to the right base, turning double plays with quickness and accuracy, and even knock balls down so that a runner simply doesn't get an extra base. There are a lot of intricacies to the job.

## *Always Be Prepared*

All players, especially infielders, ask themselves:

- How many outs?

- How many runners are on base, and what bases are they on?

- Is the runner fast or slow?

- What is the inning?

- What is the score?

- If the ball comes to me, what do I do with it?

- If the ball doesn't come to me, where do I go?

A player should think, *Okay, I've got runners on first and third. If the ball is hit to me and I've got a chance to turn a double play, I need to do that. If not, I need to cut the runner down at home plate.* This is an instantaneous decision as long as the options are thought out ahead of time.

Once the ball is hit to you, you make the decision. The worst thing for a player to do is catch the ball and then try to figure out what to do with it. By then it is too late.

## *The Corners*

Big players on both edges of the infield are expected to produce runs and provide better than adequate defense. The more they hit, the worse their defense is allowed to be. No team will settle for bad defense because there are plenty of good enough defensive players who can hit somewhat. A defensive player who can hit well is worth a lot at these two positions.

**TIPS**

The corners in the outfield (left and right field) and the infield (first and third base) are theoretically the big run-producing positions.

# First Base—Recording Outs

First basemen record the most outs of any players.

The first baseman covers first base if there is a runner on the base, and he covers the base if there is an attempted steal of second base.

**TIPS**

First basemen use whichever foot is comfortable for them to cover the bag. And the proper technique is to provide a nice big target but not to stretch in any direction until after the ball is thrown. First basemen need to be flexible so they can go get the ball wherever it is thrown. In the event that it comes down to staying on the bag or getting off the bag and getting the ball, the first baseman should always choose going for the ball.

The first baseman typically plays at about the cut of the outfield grass. If a first baseman is particularly slow, he may play a little closer to first base.

Of course, if a runner is on first base, the first baseman will play on the bag and then break off of it as the pitch is thrown. He is there to keep the runner on first base close. If he is there, the pitcher has someone to throw to to pick off the runner. The runner knows this and stays closer to the bag.

**A first baseman covers the bag when a runner is on first base.**

© Chris Hamilton, Atlanta, GA

The only other variable for a first baseman (and the same is true for a third baseman on the other line) is that he will play closer to the line later in the game. He wants to cut all chances of an extra base hit up the line late in the game.

## First Basemen at Bat

First basemen are expected to produce. This is an offensive position. Although a player with a great glove is a huge asset, a glove alone will never keep the job at first base. He often bats in the middle of the batting order. Many first basemen are cleanup hitters and appear fourth in the batting order because they are expected to drive in the most runs. (For more on the batting order, see Chapter 19.)

## Tom's Top First Basemen of the 1990s

- Andres Galarraga—A great power hitter who drives in a lot of runs and plays superb defense.

- Mark McGwire—Seventy home runs! That's all I need to say.

- Frank Thomas—The ultimate mixture of power, average, and walks. He gets on base a lot and he drives in a lot of runs.

# Third Base—The Hot Corner

Third basemen have almost no time to react. The ball is hit to them quite hard. Bang!

© Chris Hamilton, Atlanta, GA

**When a ball is hit to a third baseman, he doesn't have time to think about it. He just reacts.**

The ball comes at them like a shot and they have to react. This short reaction time is actually advantageous to some players. Some shortstops, in fact, move to third base because it's easier to react to these shots than to wait for some of the balls that come deeper to the shortstop.

**TOM'S TIPS**

Third basemen should know whether the batter might bunt. If the batter might, in fact, bunt, the third baseman will play closer to home plate to anticipate the possibility of a bunt. But, if a big power hitter comes to the plate, he does you a favor if he bunts and takes away his power threat. A power hitter will rarely if ever bunt and so a third baseman will play further back for a power hitter.

### Third Basemen at Bat

Third basemen are offensive players. Many of them are power guys, but all should be run producers—if they hit for average or for power. They appear in the middle of the batting order.

# The Middle Infield

The middle of the field is about defense. Middle infielders should bring some offense to the game, too, but this is not necessary. Players such as Nomar Garciaparra at shortstop or Roberto Alomar at second base, who provide offense and defense, are huge luxuries. But the name of the game in the middle infield is defense. That's always the first part of the job description.

# Second Base—Pivot and Jump

The specialized skill second basemen must have is the ability to turn the double play because it is such a huge defensive weapon. The key defensive play is the double play, which requires a pivot and throw. Smaller sleeker players are usually better at executing the essential acrobatics of the job. You can never say never about any position, but a typical second baseman is smaller than most players.

© Chris Hamilton, Atlanta, GA

Second basemen have to change direction right in front of the base runner when they cover second base on a double play.

Beyond turning the double play, a second baseman is supposed to catch all ground balls hit his way and cover the bag on attempted steals (unless a left-handed batter is at bat).

A second baseman is also a cutoff man for a hit to right field. He will know the ability of his right fielder and he will go out as far as necessary. When he is the cutoff man, a second baseman gauges the situation, the hit, the arm strength of his right fielder, and his own arm strength.

If, for instance, there is a runner on first base and the ball is hit to right field, the second baseman will line himself up between the ball in right field and third base.

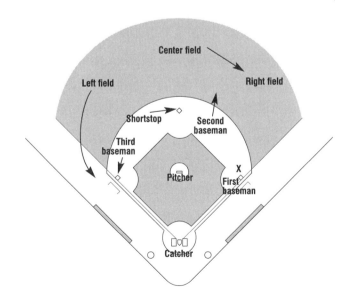

When a player goes out to catch a cutoff throw, he wants to position himself so he can best catch *and throw*. He has to throw to be an effective cutoff man. Oftentimes, a cutoff man needs to catch and then keep the ball going in the same direction (say, toward home plate). If, for instance, a player is a right-handed second baseman, he would want to turn toward his left shoulder while throwing so he could have a powerful throw. In order to do this, he would hope to find the optimal position to catch the ball and then turn and throw it. When it works, it is flawless. When it doesn't work, a second baseman wastes a lot of time getting into position after he catches the ball.

Making a cutoff work is harder than it looks. It comes from years of playing the game and understanding what you should do, as a second baseman, when the ball is hit to a certain spot in right field. You don't always have time to turn and line yourself up. You have to line yourself up based on your surroundings and where you are in relation to the field. In that instance, you have to trust everything you've learned in all those baseball games since little league and hope that you are just right.

## Second Basemen at Bat

Although second base isn't generally considered an offensive position, there are many different kinds of second basemen. There are patient, leadoff type hitters. There are contact hitters and guys who are good at the hit and run. Some are better second in the batting order than first. Others bat near the bottom of the order. They are not usually power hitters.

## *Tom's Top Second Basemen of the 1990s*

- Roberto Alomar—An ideal leadoff hitter who hits for average and some power and is a tremendous defensive player. He is very smart—a highlight reel type of player.

- Craig Biggio—He is also a tremendous leadoff hitter who hits for average and takes a lot of walks. He has some power and can steal bases. And, he is a great fielder.

- Chuck Knoblauch—Another great leadoff hitter who plays great defense.

# *Shortstop—Saving Runs*

The most challenging and important position to play on defense is shortstop.

**Shortstops are asked routinely to make great plays.**

© Chris Hamilton, Atlanta, GA

A shortstop gets a lot of chances, so he is there to make the most of those chances. First, he is a defensive player. Although there are exceptions to every rule, over the years shortstop has been the one position where teams have traditionally sacrificed offense for good defense. Frankly, many shortstops haven't been good hitters. But they are *expected* to play stellar defense.

**TOM'S TIPS**

When a shortstop goes deep in the hole and makes a great play, his pitcher is quite happy. That's one less out needed. And every pitcher knows that a lot can happen before any certain out. So, every out is great and ones that you don't expect are especially sweet.

Shortstops do what second basemen do. They take cutoff throws from the outfield. They cover second base on steals when a left-handed batter is up. They turn double plays.

## Shortstops at Bat

Shortstops of recent vintage have been getting bigger and more powerful, but the big powerful shortstop is still the exception. Most shortstops are smaller guys who are defensive wizards and have some offensive ability. Of course, some guys can hit better than others. But generally, shortstops are in the game to play defense.

### *Tom's Top Three Shortstops of the 1990s*

- Barry Larkin—A good all-around mixture of offense and defense. He is a really smart player who has great range and hands on defense. On offense, he hits for average and has great speed.

- Cal Ripken—Mr. Consistency. A manager could pencil Cal in for 162 games a year for more than a decade. That is incredibly comforting, especially since Mr. Consistency brings along the great numbers. He has a mixture of everything.

- Alex Rodriguez—An atypical shortstop. He is almost too good. He's a great fluid shortstop and puts up numbers that would make a left fielder proud. He has size, power, and defense.

# Catcher—Inside the Pulse of the Game

Behind the plate, the catcher is in the middle of every play. He sets the target for the pitcher.

Of course, a catcher does more than just stick out his glove. He calls the game and he is expected to catch all pitched balls, even the ones in the dirt, and he is supposed to throw out runners attempting to steal bases. In addition, catchers cover all plays at home plate. They field bunts that stop near the plate and they back up first base on ground balls that are throwouts when no one else is on base.

I want a catcher who can hit.

Theoretically, I think that a good catcher can produce more runs with his bat than he can save with his arm. Certainly, a catcher who can call a good game is valuable. It saves a pitcher a lot of aggravation. But if a catcher can hit, I'll take him.

Some catchers are better behind the plate than others. When calling a game, a catcher must know his pitcher and know what that pitcher likes to do in certain situations. If a catcher knows a pitcher's strengths, he has some reference points. If a pitcher feels the catcher understands, he can explain some basic strategy ahead of time. For instance, if a pitcher shakes off one kind of pitch, the catcher will choose another so the pitcher can get to where he wants to be.

**A catcher wants to know how a pitcher plans to approach a batter.**

© Chris Hamilton, Atlanta, GA

Some pitchers and catchers talk to each other more than others do. I am probably on the lower end of needing a conversation, since my strategy is pretty clear to everyone—even the batter. My catcher knows I am not out to exploit the other guy's weakness but to stay within my strength. Greg Maddux probably has more conversations with catchers because his approach is more complex. But in baseball, the approach doesn't count. The results do.

## Blocking Balls

This is an overlooked skill, yet it is incredibly important. Blocking balls often translates into the confidence of a pitcher. If a pitcher is afraid of a catcher's ability to block a ball in the dirt, he may be afraid to throw a curve ball in an important situation with men on base. And, if he can't use all his pitches, he won't be as effective.

The technique of blocking balls often doesn't even involve the glove. It simply calls for the catcher to slide his crouched body in front of the ball so it bounces off of him and ends up on the ground in front of him. That's blocking—just knocking it down.

## Catchers at Bat

Catchers should hit. These guys usually aren't great runners because they crouch too much to be fast.

## *Tom's Top Catchers of the 1990s*

- Charles Johnson—He breaks the rule on wanting an offensive catcher because he really doesn't bring a lot of offense. But he is so dominating on defense that you can't help but notice him.

- Mike Piazza—Just the opposite of Johnson. Piazza is an offensive powerhouse who sacrifices a little on defense. But gosh, who cares? He crushes the ball.

- Ivan Rodriguez—A great offensive catcher who has an arm that frightens base runners. He is the complete package.

# *Pitchers on Defense*

Pitchers really like it when the ball is hit on the ground, so most pitchers try to lure the hitter to hit there. If the ball is hit it is usually hit on the ground. Four players, plus the pitcher and catcher, play in close enough to field these ground balls and convert them into outs.

The pitcher wants another player to catch the ball. But sometimes, he's the guy. He does more than just throw pitches. Pitchers are infielders.

Pitchers have to cut down balls hit up the middle. Pitchers can help corner men at first and third base by chasing balls along the line that are not hit hard.

The biggest problem for a pitcher on defense is forgetting that the ball could be hit straight at him. You just hope it doesn't happen. If it does you hope (A) you are quick enough to react, or (B) if it hits you it hits you in

a muscle area and not a bone area—and certainly not in the head. Other than that, you just don't think about it.

# Three Outfielders and Their Bats

## CHAPTER NINE

**A PIECE OF WOOD SMACKING A FASTBALL INTO THE AIR** can really send it a long way. But most times when the ball is hit in the air, the batter doesn't get "all" of it. Instead of going over the fence, the ball falls somewhere on the green expanse in front of the fence. Three guys cover that ground. They are outfielders.

Most balls are hit to the infield. But every game, every pitcher, every batter, and every pitch is different. Some pitchers throw more pitches hit as fly balls than others do. Although a great majority of all hit balls are plays for the infield, there are usually key plays for the outfield during any game. Key plays happen in the outfield because a ball hit *that* far, even though it did not go over the fence, can cause a lot of damage if it isn't caught. It could fall anywhere on the large green expanse in front of the fence.

The fence can be 400 or more feet from home plate in deep center field. If the ball is hit out to deep center and bounces around, a fast runner can go a long way around the bases. Outfielders don't receive nearly as many baseballs as infielders. But balls hit out there are very dangerous.

# Center Field Rules

The center fielder is the captain of the outfield. He goes for anything he can get to and waves off the other fielders if he thinks he has the best chance at it. Center fielders are quick and have a great ability to get to the ball. Look at any outfield, even a small outfield, and you will see that there is a lot of ground to cover.

## Center Fielders at Bat

Center field is a defensive position. Usually, center fielders are good hitters and great base runners. Often, they are leadoff hitters—first at bat for their team in the game.

Some center fielders are powerful hitters and appear third or fourth in the batting order (more on the batting order in Chapter 19). But typically a center fielder is a less powerful player with a lot of speed. Once in a while, teams get lucky and find a center fielder with a mix of power and speed (such as Ken Griffey Jr.).

## Deep or Shallow

Most center fielders will play deep to make sure nothing gets over their heads. But some center fielders play in shallow to steal away bloop hits (which, to a pitcher, are like Chinese water torture). They can only play shallow if they are able to go back and catch long fly balls.

**HOW IT HAPPENED**

In the 1954 World Series, Willie Mays of the New York Giants went straight back in center field on a long shot hit by Vic Wertz of the Cleveland Indians and he snagged it and threw it in. The Giants went on to beat the heavily favored Indians and many still point to "The Catch" as the turning point of the series.

A center fielder's starting position depends on his ability to go back on the ball. It is clearly more important to be able to catch balls hit behind him than it is to get to the ones hit in front of him, because those long shots, if not caught, can cause more damage.

## Robbing a Run

A spectacular leaping-over-the-fence catch can destroy an offense. Although most outfielders can make this play (except those fielders who

play in places such as left field at Fenway Park—where the fence is 35 feet high—try leaping over that), center fielders perform this feat more often. Players like Ken Griffey Jr. or my former teammate Kenny Lofton can demoralize a team that thinks it has scored one or more runs by making this play.

© MLB Photos

When an outfielder leaps over the fence and steals away a home run, it energizes his team and demoralizes the other team.

## Tom's Top Three Center Fielders of the 1990s

- Ken Griffey Jr.—Probably the best baseball player of our generation. He can literally do it all and he does it all with flair. An incredible Gold Glove fielder with astonishing speed, Griffey brings the biggest lumber in the American League to bat—smacking fifty-six home runs last year.

• Kenny Lofton—A prototypical center fielder/leadoff hitter. He combines speed and great instincts, both offensively on the bases and defensively in the field. He can intimidate a pitcher with his base running and he has shown great instinct for the dramatic, over-the-fence home run-robbing catch.

• Bernie Williams—He quietly won the American League batting championship on a team that won more games than any team in history. He plays a flawless, gliding center field and is a prolific hitter.

# Left Field—Making Routine Plays and Hitting Big

Most batters are right-handed and therefore hit the ball straight when they turn on the ball and send it to left field. This makes the flight of the ball "true," unlike in right field where the ball soars off a right-hander's bat with a spin. Thus the job of the left fielder is a bit more routine than the other two outfield positions. He is expected to catch all the balls hit to him, help cut off gaps (more later), and hit the cutoff man with his throws to the infield. Spectacular plays on defense are a bonus because his job is to catch what he is supposed to catch. Left fielders are offensive players.

## Left Fielders at Bat

A left fielder drives in runs, hits home runs, and generally provides a threatening presence in the batting order. He usually hits somewhere in

the middle of the batting order and brings some brawn and power to the plate.

### Tom's Top Three Left Fielders of the 1990s

- Albert Belle—He just puts up huge numbers. All season long, every season, he is productive. I have noticed that every season he seems to go on a two-month tear that is almost impossible to comprehend. He does it every year. He can carry a team when he gets hot.

- Barry Bonds—He is a great defensive left fielder who doesn't have a great arm. Instead, he has great instincts. And, offensively, he is as good as anybody. He's the only guy in the history of baseball with 400 steals and 400 home runs. He does it all.

- Joe Carter—Mr. RBI. He has an uncanny ability to get base runners around the bases. Plus, as a Toronto Blue Jay he hit a dramatic home run off Philadelphia Phillie reliever Mitch Williams to win the 1993 World Series.

# Right Fielders—Big Arms and Good Range

A right fielder has a tougher job than a left fielder because a ball coming off a right-hander's bat will fly out to right field with a slicing action and a weird spin. This makes fly balls tougher to "read." And, since the center fielder will often shift toward left field, the right fielder often has more range to cover than the left fielder does.

The other key ingredient of a right fielder is a big arm, because he has a longer throw to make key plays at third base than a left fielder does. If a right fielder has a big arm and the other team knows it, runners are often afraid to advance on him. Some right fielders intimidate players by their presence and the reputation of their arm.

## Right Fielders at Bat

Run production is important in right field. Right fielders often bat in the middle of the batting order and hit either with power or a high average and speed. Right fielders are expected to be offensive players.

## Tom's Top Right Fielders of the 1990s

- Juan Gonzales—This run-producing machine of the Texas Rangers has an ability to dominate for long stretches at a time. He is a force.

- Tony Gwynn—He may be the smartest hitter in baseball. Tony is always making adjustments and owns a slew of batting titles *and* Gold Gloves.

- Sammy Sosa—He hit sixty-six home runs in 1998! And, he has a strong, accurate arm and makes all the plays he is supposed to make. He is an all-around great player.

# *Working Together and Closing Gaps*

An outfield is a big area for three players to cover. Pitchers know it and so do batters. Batters see gaps between the players. These gaps are places batters try to hit the ball to because they figure that the outfielders cannot get to the ball in the gap before it falls to the ground. Sometimes, they are right.

But a good outfielder often catches a ball in a gap. The key is to get a good jump on the ball.

**If a player gets a good jump on the ball, he can help his team a lot.**

© Chris Hamilton, Atlanta, GA

Often, a fielder knows what a pitcher is trying to do to a hitter and will anticipate where the ball will be hit. Of course, an outfielder can anticipate that one kind of pitch will be thrown and, if a pitcher throws a completely different pitch, the hit ball will move in a completely different way.

When a fielder is heading in the right direction at the time the ball is hit, that's a jump. Then he must recognize the flight of the ball. Some of this is instinct and some is learned, but the only way to get better is to practice. The more fly balls you catch, the more you will learn.

A jump is important because, beyond executing routine plays, outfielders must catch balls hit in the gap. If a ball is hit in the gap between two outfielders, it can roll for a long time. Although the spectacular catch over the fence gets a lot of attention, balls cut off in the gap save many more runs. More balls are hit in gaps than over the fence. When an outfielder gets to one of those gap shots, he holds a batter to a single instead of a double or maybe a triple. That's huge.

**TOM'S TIPS**

Players know when to dive. They know if they have a chance or if it is futile. If a player thinks he has a chance and that he will be backed up he will most likely go for it. If it is late in the game, he may err on the side of caution. But if it is a do or die situation, he will go for it as hard as he can even if he is pretty sure he doesn't have it.

Players also study the tendencies of batters and can "cheat" a little— meaning they lean in a certain direction as the pitch comes.

# The Cutoff Throw

Certain plays make a difference. Sometimes outfielders must decide whether to try to tag out a runner going to a base or throw the ball low enough so it can be caught by a cutoff man. There just aren't many guys who can throw a ball on a line—forehead high to a cutoff man—and have it carry to the base. Most have to throw with more of an arc for a throw to get to the base. These players have to make a decision about hitting the cutoff man before they throw it.

Smart decisions help win baseball games.

© Chris Hamilton, Atlanta, GA

Outfielders have to try to make a throw long enough to get to a base and yet low enough to be cut off if necessary. The cutoff man is in line between the outfielder and the base.

# The Fundamentals

## CHAPTER TEN

**BASEBALL IS A MENTAL GAME.** Baseball players must understand certain *fundamentals* and execute them efficiently in order to be good baseball players. Fundamental baseball includes the ability to field the ball and catch it, find and hit a cutoff man with a throw, back up bases, bunt, hit and run, and turn a double play. Essentially, playing fundamental baseball means playing smart baseball.

Fundamental baseball in action requires no mental errors. A mental error occurs when a player loses focus on the game and doesn't do something he is supposed to do. Most often in the major leagues, however, a mental error occurs when a player tries to do too much and suddenly forgets to do something basic.

## THE TWO MOST IMPORTANT FUNDAMENTALS

- Hustle—mentally and physically.
- Keep your eyes on the ball.

# Concentration

Concentration has a lot to do with preparation. Hitters go up to bat with an idea of where they want to hit the ball and an idea of what they are looking for in a pitch. Beyond that, the batter must concentrate on the task at hand.

A fielder is ready before the ball is hit his way. In fact, before every pitch, a fielder reviews in his mind how many outs there are and how many runners are on base. Most importantly, before every pitch a fielder asks himself, *If the ball is hit to me, what am I going to do with it?*

Although all players are liable to make a physical mistake—miss the ball, make a bad throw, etc.—mental mistakes can kill a team. A mental error is simply a matter of not being prepared.

# Catching and Throwing

The fundamental defensive skill in baseball is catching the ball and then throwing it.

# *Ground Balls*

Fielding position is key to catching a ground ball. If you don't have it, you are in trouble. Stand on the balls of your feet with your knees bent and your glove in front of you. Your feet should be shoulder-width apart so you can move in any direction as quickly as possible. Keep your chin down to force yourself to keep your eyes on the ball until it lands in your glove. If you are back on your heels or if your glove is under your butt, you will be out of position and your movements will be restricted.

© Chris Hamilton, Atlanta, GA

**It is important to balance and keep your eyes on the ball until it falls into your glove.**

# *Throwing*

Throw the ball at a teammate's chest to give him the best chance to make the play.

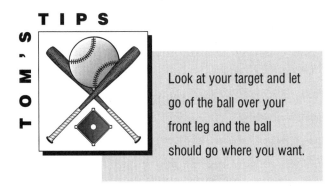

**TIPS**

**TOM'S**

Look at your target and let go of the ball over your front leg and the ball should go where you want.

Though each player's physical build makes his throw different from everyone else's, all players must plant their back foot and stride toward the player they are throwing to to guarantee accuracy and power.

# *Catching Flies*

Catching a fly ball hit to you is harder than catching a ball thrown to you. You need to learn how the ball comes off the bat and the only way to learn is to catch a lot of fly balls. By the time a player has made it to the major leagues, he has caught thousands of fly balls in his life, yet you will still see him misjudge balls from time to time. This gives you an idea of how hard it is to catch a fly.

Usually, you have to make the right decision as soon as the ball is hit in order to have a chance to catch it. You have to judge where it is going.

**Learning to judge the distance of fly balls takes practice.**

© Chris Hamilton, Atlanta, GA

You might master catching the ball from 50 feet, but if you are 100 feet away it is a completely different situation—the ball is up in the air and wind longer and you are looking up at it for a longer period of time.

Moving left or right, coming in or going back—it's a judgment call. Every fly ball is different and no matter how well players catch them, they find they are better in certain positions and play the field accordingly. Of course, positioning also depends on the other fielders, the batter, the pitch thrown, and where the ball is hit.

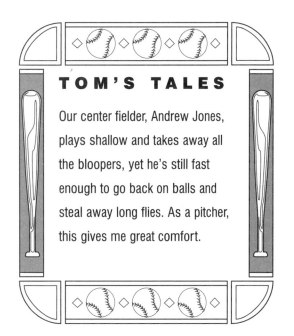

### TOM'S TALES

Our center fielder, Andrew Jones, plays shallow and takes away all the bloopers, yet he's still fast enough to go back on balls and steal away long flies. As a pitcher, this gives me great comfort.

Most outfielders are better at coming in on a ball than going out, so most outfielders play deep. But if an outfielder can go back for the ball, he can play in close and catch a lot of bloopers that would normally fall for hits.

The best thing for a young player to do is to learn to catch a straight-on short fly first and then work on further distances from there.

# *Defensive Positioning and Why Players Shift*

Each player covers a general area in the infield or outfield.

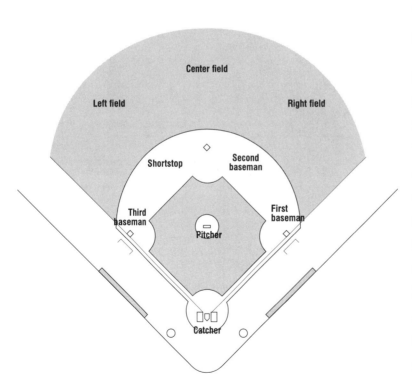

These are the places players normally play on defense.

Players shift in the field somewhat, depending on the situation and the batter. The bench coach (more on coaches in Chapter 20) decides how to move players about the field. Every player looks to the bench to see where they'll be. The most important positions—the ones that will shift—are the center fielder, the shortstop, and the first and third basemen.

The center fielder will shift either to the shortstop side of the outfield or the to second baseman's side. The shortstop will shift one way or another, based on a hitter's tendencies and the pitcher. The two corner infielders, the first baseman and the third baseman, will guard the lines late in the game. Although their chances of catching everything decrease when they guard the line, they must catch the ball down the line that could be at least a double if it gets past them.

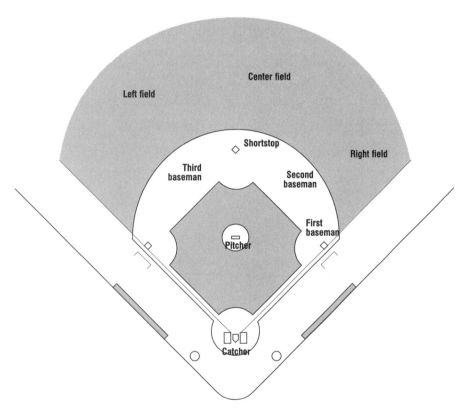

THE BONDS SHIFT: The Braves drastically shift positions when Barry Bonds comes up to bat because we know this three-time MVP is going to pull the ball. So we play without a third baseman. We move our third baseman to the shortstop position and we put our shortstop right behind second base. Then the second baseman is near first base and the first baseman is right on the line. Even with this shift, Barry still pulls the ball because he is confident doing what he does best.

# *Hitting Cutoff Men*

If the ball is hit into the outfield and is bouncing around, the outfielder must pick it up and then throw it into the infield. He does not just throw it to any infielder. He throws it to a specific place, depending on the situation.

Some throws are easier than other throws. Throwing the ball into second is much easier than trying to throw a runner out at the plate while at the same time throwing it low enough to be cut off. It is hard enough trying to throw the runner out at the plate, but hitting the cutoff man and still throwing a good ball to the plate is a real challenge. But good ballplayers can do it.

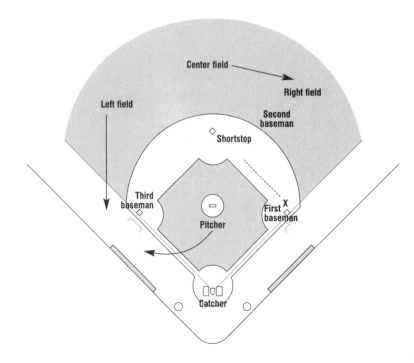

If you have a runner on first base and the ball is hit to right field, the second baseman will be the cutoff man, lined up between the ball and third base. The shortstop covers second base. In that situation, the pitcher is probably backing up home plate. The left fielder will back up third base.

I think hitting the cutoff man is a lost art because it doesn't make the high-light shows anymore. You are not going to see a player hitting a cutoff man on ESPN's SportsCenter. It's not a highlight. It's a fundamental.

It's funny. You can go to a game and see an outfielder just air out a throw all the way to home, and even if the runner is safe, the crowd cheers. Nobody cheers if the throw is cut off. So a player often hears those cheers and thinks it's a great thing to throw the ball as far as he can.

Maybe he occasionally does something great like scaring a runner from going all the way home. His big throw may have gotten the runner out. But for every one time that a big throw without regard to the cutoff man *works*, it *doesn't work* about ten times.

Let's say there is a runner at first and the ball is hit to right field. If the right fielder just airs it out to get the runner going to third, he may get him. But more likely he won't and then the batter who hit the ball will go all the way to second. If the ball were cut off, the runner would be forced to stay at first. There is a big difference between having runners at first and third base, and having them at second and third base. If there is a runner at first, you can make a double play. If there is no runner at first, you have to walk a batter to create a force situation.

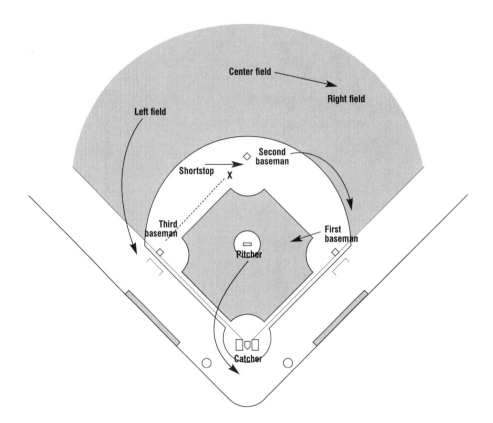

When there is a runner at second base and the ball is hit to right field, there is a potential play at the plate. In this situation, the right fielder's job is to throw the ball to home in order to get the runner out. But he must also throw it on a low enough line drive so that somebody can cut it off if the runner is going to score anyway. The purpose of a cutoff is to get a chance to tag out the batter who is now most likely running to second base. So a cutoff and a quick throw to second would nail the runner. But this is only done if the throw to home does not have a chance of preventing the run.

On a play at the plate, the cutoff man is generally the third baseman for any ball hit from left field to center field, and the first baseman is the cutoff man for any ball hit from center field to right field. Generally, if it is early in the game, he will cut off the throw and get the batter running to second for the sure out. If it is late and the runner coming home could make the deciding run in the game, he's probably going to take the chance and let the ball go to the plate.

## Turning a Double Play

Talk about a defensive weapon. If you can turn a double play and get two outs with one hit ball, you often wipe out a potential rally. Therefore, for infielders, this is a fundamental skill.

There are many types of double plays, but the most common and fundamental happens when a runner is on first base and the batter hits a ground ball to the infield. The double play is simply a transfer of the ball from the player who fielded it, to the player covering second base for a force out, to the first baseman to get the batter out.

Turning a double play requires a bit of courage by a second baseman.

© Chris Hamilton, Atlanta, GA

If you watch a successful double play combination between shortstop and second baseman—which is the most common—you will notice that they are able to transfer the ball from glove to hand to glove to hand seamlessly. The toss of the ball from the fielder to the player covering second is often an underhand flip because a hard overhand throw from a short distance could be impossible to catch. As much as you want to be quick, you don't want to sacrifice accuracy for quickness; you can be much more accurate on a short toss with an underhand throw. Plus, it is easier to see. The player fielding the ball will try to aim the ball to the player covering second base somewhere between the hips and chest.

**TOM'S TIPS**

Good baseball players always make their teammates' jobs easier, and that is especially true of the double-play second-base ball transfer. The guy throwing the baseball is supposed to make it as easy as possible for the guy who catches it.

The player covering the base must have the ball in his hand when he steps on second base, and he will force out the runner if the ball beats him there. Then the player covering the base has to throw it to first base.

If the ball is hit to the shortstop side of the infield, the second baseman covers second base. But if the ball is hit to the second base side of the infield, the shortstop covers second base. A second baseman has to virtually pivot on one foot and change direction as he goes from catching to throwing. And while he does this, the runner from first is barreling in on him.

From a runner's perspective, when you are going to be out at second base anyway, you still run as hard as you can and you slide. The whole idea at that point is to disrupt the throw. Sometimes it works.

# Rundowns

Every once in a while, a runner gets caught between bases. When the defense catches a runner between bases, they want to force him to run back to the base he started from and make a play as he hustles back. It is important to make the runner commit to the base he ran from so that even if he is safe, he hasn't made it to the next base.

The player with the ball should hold it up as he chases the runner so that his teammate can see it and make an easy catch if he throws it.

Lots of players are involved in a rundown. In the most common scenario, the pitcher will throw to first base when the runner is leaning toward second. Then the runner is caught in the middle. The first baseman has the ball and the runner is between him and the second baseman. The pitcher backs up first base; the shortstop backs up second base. The catcher runs to first base and takes the place of the pitcher because fielders, rather than pitchers, should handle the ball when possible. In addition, the right fielder and center fielder could back up the rundown and the left fielder could back up any possible play at third base.

More than two fielders are involved in the rundown because, if the runner gets past one of the fielders, the player with the ball can throw it to a fielder behind him. Fielders might throw the ball back and forth a number

of times if the runner is smart and quick; but they try to keep the number of throws to a minimum and force the runner back to his original base.

# Batting

Every batter is different, but batting is about balance and timing.

It all starts with balance. Some guys have a wider stance, meaning that they stand with their legs wider than shoulder-width apart—sometimes a lot more. Some guys have a narrower stance. Some guys have their bats and backs up elbow-high. Others are down low. Some guys stand up straight; others crouch like they are about to sit down. The individual decides. That's the beauty of baseball. Good players are smart enough to figure out what works for them. But if you don't have good balance, you don't have a good chance of being successful.

After balance, batting is about looking at the ball. You have to see the ball. If you don't see the ball, forget it.

# The Swing

The best swing is a level swing. Don't swing up. Don't swing down. When a player swings, he wants to think about hitting the middle of the ball right up the middle of the field. Step at the pitcher with the front foot while keeping the back foot planted firmly on the ground.

My old teammate David Justice, who now plays for the Cleveland Indians, has one of the nicest, most balanced swings around.

© Chris Hamilton, Atlanta, GA

# Strategic Hitting

Hitters theoretically hit the ball where it is pitched. If the pitcher threw the ball outside to a right-handed hitter, the batter will try to hit it to right field. And, if the ball is pitched inside, near the hitter, he will try to pull it to left field.

But not all hitters do that. Tony Gwynn of the San Diego Padres can hit the ball inside out, meaning he can send an inside pitch to right field by leading his swing with his hands instead of with the barrel of the bat.

Of course, not everybody is Tony Gwynn. Some players are such dead pull hitters that they have a very difficult time hitting the ball to the opposite field.

## The Sacrifice Fly

If there is a runner on third base with less than two outs, a batter merely has to hit the ball deep to the outfield so the runner can score if he tags his base after the catch. Generally, most outfielders are not going to throw out a runner in this situation.

Different hitters have different theories about hitting a sacrifice fly. Some say if you go up to bat trying to hit a fly ball in this situation, it's easy to pop up. Others look at this as an easy RBI. But remember, the pitcher knows it is an easy RBI and is probably throwing the ball low to try to keep all hit balls on the ground.

## The Hit and Run

From a batter's perspective, trying to hit in a hit and run situation is a difficult assignment that *must* be executed. If the batter fails, it's not a hit and run—it's just a dead-duck runner.

The idea of this play (which will be described in more detail in Chapter 21) is for the runner to wait a little longer than he normally would to steal and then take off. Then it's up to the hitter to hit the ball. If he does, the runner should make it to second and may make it to third, if the batter hit a good shot to right field.

# Hitting Behind the Runner

If there is a runner on second base and nobody out, a hitter may hit the ball to the right side of the field—behind the runner. The reason to do this is that once the ball is caught it is a longer throw to third base and the runner can advance. The first priority in this situation is to get the ball on the ground. A team will sacrifice an out in order to move the runner to third base. If the ball happens to get through the infield, the runner can score all the way from second base on that play.

# Trying to Hit a Home Run

In certain situations, you need a home run. A power hitter might come up and try to hit a home run. But this is not a common occurrence. After hitting a home run, most home run hitters will usually say that they were just trying to hit the ball hard.

If the situation calls for it and a power hitter is up, he will try to whack it over the fence. For instance, if you are down by two runs with two runners on base and two outs, the big guy is swinging for a home run to win the game. And it happens.

# *Bunting*

The batter bunts when he hits a short little ground ball that stops rolling less than halfway to first or third base. The bunt is a weapon used to advance runners when there are no outs or, in some cases, when there is one out. The bunt is essentially a sacrifice because usually the defensive team can throw out the batter on a bunt.

A well-executed bunt is one that is also well-thought-out. The runner knows about it ahead of time, so he is ready to take off as soon as the ball is bunted. It is up to the batter to hit it correctly. If he makes a mistake and pops it up, he is out. Following this mistake, if the runner doesn't get back to his original base before the defensive team catches the ball and throws it to that base, then he is out, too.

The bunt *must* be hit on the ground. A right-handed batter holds the bottom of the bat with his left hand and then slides his right hand up the barrel of the bat as the pitch comes in. Then he turns his body so he is almost facing the pitcher. The key is to keep the barrel of the bat above the handle. Hold the bat firmly with your bottom hand in order to bunt the ball hard. If your bottom hand grips the bat loosely, you will cushion the blow and the ball will die close to the plate.

# The Show, The Major Leagues

**THERE IS A CERTAIN PINCH-ME QUALITY** about playing in the major leagues. I know, I think all professional baseball players know how great it really is. We all remember many teammates and friends from our past who didn't make it. We remember going to games ourselves or watching on television. And now—I am that guy on TV.

Part Four tells how the major leagues work. I explain the dynamics of the long season as it builds up to the playoffs and the World Series. And, since baseball is clearly a business, I briefly delve into that aspect of the game. Finally, I will talk about the system that feeds players into the major leagues—the minor leagues.

# Organizing the Best in the World

## CHAPTER ELEVEN

**MILLIONS OF PEOPLE ACROSS THE WORLD PLAY BASEBALL**, yet there are only 750 spots open in the major leagues. Major league baseball is the place where all the best baseball players from around the globe gather to play. It is a melting pot of astonishing talent.

Baseball has its own system of organization. For instance, the thirty teams in baseball are divided into two leagues—an *American League* and a *National League*. And players from all over the world become members of these teams in different ways.

## *How to Become an Atlanta Brave*

In America, players are drafted. The Atlanta Braves drafted me in the second round in 1984. I was the forty-fifth player chosen that year.

Young American players who have graduated from high school or who are at least juniors in college are eligible for the annual draft. The team with the worst record picks first. There are more than 100 rounds, and more than 2,000 players are drafted every year. (More on the levels of professional baseball below the major leagues in Chapter 13.) When a team drafts you, you are only allowed to negotiate with that team (more on the business of the game in Chapter 14).

Young players from other countries are free agents—they can negotiate with any team. In the Dominican Republic, some major league baseball teams have set up leagues to help develop players. Great baseball players come from all around the world, and pockets of talent thrive all across America. In the old days, it was possible for the big clubs to miss a talented player. But because of expansion, there are opportunities—more teams equal more jobs.

Players are also traded (sometimes two for one, or five for two) just like pieces of property.

But players also have rights. When a player has played for more than six years and is not under contract, he is allowed to negotiate with all teams. Then he is a free agent (see Chapter 14).

# *The Basic Setup*

In major league baseball, thirty teams comprise two leagues and each team plays a 162-game regular season. At the end of each season, there is a championship called the World Series.

The World Series is a seven-game challenge match in which the champion of the *National League* and the champion of the *American League* play a series of games until one team wins four games.

Trimming those thirty teams into the two that compete in the World Series is a bit more involved than simply playing out the season. Each league has playoff games that occur after the season and prior to the World Series.

Okay... specifically...

The National League consists of sixteen teams and the American League has fourteen teams. Each League has three geographic divisions: the East Division, the Central Division, and the West Division. At the end of the season, the team in each division that wins the most games is the champion of that division.

The wild card team from each league is the one second-place team among the three divisions that has the best record.

So, four teams in each league make the playoffs: the champions of each of the three divisions and the wild card team. (See Chapter 13 for more on the playoffs and World Series.)

Here is how baseball is organized:

| NATIONAL LEAGUE | AMERICAN LEAGUE |
| --- | --- |

**EAST DIVISION**

| NATIONAL LEAGUE | AMERICAN LEAGUE |
| --- | --- |
| Atlanta Braves | Baltimore Orioles |
| Florida Marlins | Boston Red Sox |
| New York Mets | New York Yankees |
| Philadelphia Phillies | Tampa Bay Devil Rays |
| Montreal Expos | Toronto Blue Jays |

**CENTRAL DIVISION**

| | |
| --- | --- |
| Chicago Cubs | Chicago White Sox |
| Cincinnati Reds | Cleveland Indians |
| Houston Astros | Detroit Tigers |
| Milwaukee Brewers | Kansas City Royals |
| Pittsburgh Pirates | Minnesota Twins |
| St. Louis Cardinals | |

**WEST DIVISION**

| | |
| --- | --- |
| Arizona Diamondbacks | Anaheim Angels |
| Colorado Rockies | Oakland Athletics |
| Los Angeles Dodgers | Seattle Mariners |
| San Francisco Giants | Texas Rangers |
| San Diego Padres | |

Teams from the same general areas of the country are in the same divisions together. This is done for a number of reasons, but mostly to encourage rivalry between nearby cities. Games between cities that are rivals—especially ones within driving distance of each other—are

exciting. But besides geographic location, rivalries need history. If something dramatic occurs one year or one game or one series, both teams will remember it.

## *Trading, Signing, and Drafting— How Teams Are Put Together*

Teams acquire players in three ways:

- Drafting players through the amateur draft
- Signing free agents
- Trading for players

All teams are different. Most teams now concentrate more on developing their own players and keeping them than acquiring free agents. From time to time, teams will sign a free agent or two to bolster their nucleus of players. The main reason is economics. Although it can appear to be a quick fix to sign a bunch of superstar free agents and try to make them a team, it is clear that this is by no means foolproof. Sure, it worked once. The Florida Marlins won a championship in 1997, but the team was split up before the next season.

Most teams start with a nucleus of young players because it is easier for a team to build from within the organization. By the time a player has made the big leagues, he has probably been in the organization for two or three years. He plays minor league baseball (more in chapter 15) for the organization at higher and higher levels until he reaches the big leagues,

and along the way, he learns how the organization works—and that is significant.

And then there are trades. Being involved in a trade is very strange for a player. Suddenly, you are sent to a different city. Unlike a job transfer, you don't work for the same company. You work for a competitor. Trading is an interesting and successful way to quickly change the makeup of your team.

In general, a team wants a mix of players to avoid falling apart after one year. If you have a team of thirty-year-old players who are all free agents at the same time, there is no way you can afford to keep all of those guys together. So, in order to minimize yearly negotiations, a team should have players of various ages with varying amounts of service time (more on the business of baseball in Chapter 14).

## *What Kind of Team?—How Teams Are Built*

You want a mix.

That is the best way to describe the strategy of any baseball team—even (and especially) those built with a certain strategy in mind. The mix is the key. If you have a team built on speed, you still need some power. If you have a team of all singles hitters, you have to string together a bunch of singles to get a run. That's hard, so you try to mix in some power. If you have a team built with power, you still want guys who hit for average to be on base for your big sluggers. And all teams need to be strong defensively

up the middle. You need good pitchers too, because good pitching beats good hitting.

A team can literally ride a hot pitcher to a World Series if it plays well enough during the season to make the playoffs. That's why the playoffs are such a roll of the dice. If you were a great team but you ran into Orel Hershiser in the Fall of 1988, you were immobilized. Bob Gibson had the same impact in the 1960s. It happens. A great pitcher can have the roll of his life at just the right time. A pitcher just does his job. Some great pitchers seem to force themselves into history with pure willpower and talent. Orel Hershiser was nearly impossible to score on in late 1988. Another pitcher, Jack Morris of the Minnesota Twins, dominated my team in the 1991 World Series.

## *The 25-Man Roster*

There are eight starters in the field – 8 players

Catcher
First Baseman
Second Baseman
Shortstop
Third Baseman
Left Fielder
Center Fielder
Right Fielder

There are players on the bench to back up the starters. A utility player is one who can play more than one position well.

| | |
|---|---|
| Backup catcher | 1 player |
| Two utility infielders | 2 players |
| Two utility outfielders | 2 players |
| | |
| One player may be either a utility infielder or a utility outfielder. | 1 player |
| | |
| Five starting pitchers | 5 players |
| One closer | 1 player |
| Two left-handed relievers | 2 players |
| Three right-handed relievers | 3 players |
| | |
| TOTAL: | 25 players |

But the above alignment is *flexible*.

Some teams will keep an extra outfielder instead of an extra infielder. Some teams will only keep ten pitchers so they can keep an extra utility player. Some teams make that extra utility player a third catcher.

## *Setting Your Rotation*

Ideally, the five starting pitchers are a mix of right-handers and left-handers. But since there are more right-handed pitchers, many staffs don't have more than one left-handed starter. Some don't have any. But ideally you want one or two in order to give opposing teams a different

look. If all a team faces when they play you is right-handed pitchers, hitters can more easily zone in because they don't have to make as many adjustments.

# Making Changes to Your Team

It is always important to bring new blood to your team. Every year in the off season this is true. Of the twenty-five guys who finished the year with your club, some will leave. Some may retire. Some may file for free agency. Some may not be asked back by the club. And some may be traded for other players. Teams, even championship teams, revamp a little every year.

**TOM'S TIPS**

No one is guaranteed to do what they did last year. Some players might have a better year in the future. Others may go downhill. You don't know. So, teams have a person in charge called a general manager, and he makes the guesses.

Players in the minor leagues often have a ton of talent but need to be seasoned a bit. For a lot less money than a veteran player makes, these young hungry guys are often asked to come to the major leagues and do the same job. Sometimes they do the job better than the veteran player does. Sometimes they are worse. But now, teams are more often turning to young players to fill bench roles because they cost less money.

Saving money is important to general managers because they spend so much of it. The pressure is intense because they are in charge of handing out multi-million dollar guaranteed contracts. If a player suddenly becomes terrible, the team must pay the money. If the player gets injured, the team must pay the money.

General managers try to be careful about spending the big money on free agents. If spent on the right players, it is worth it. But mistakes are made. If a player has a 25 million dollar contract for five years, that team is stuck with that player at that price for the full five years. Thus trading becomes more difficult because trades are made on a financial basis as well as on a talent basis.

Occasionally in the past, once-successful players could be traded if they were in the midst of a bad year. Other teams would gamble that the player needed to be in a new situation to find his old skills again. This kind of trade happens less now because a player making a big check is just too big of a gamble for many teams.

Today, a high-priced player having a big year for a bad team is often traded to a good team in exchange for young prospects. In the past, a team would try to build around a superstar. Now, most try to build with youth before attracting any free agents.

During the season, teams also make changes. Sometimes a key player gets hurt or is having a bad year. Sometimes teams feel a need for a specific type of player (i.e., left-handed power hitter), and all teams always need more pitchers.

# *Trade Deadline*

Teams are allowed to make trades during the season up until July 31. After July 31, any player who might be traded is put on a waiver wire. This means that after July 31, trades can be blocked.

## HOW IT WORKS

After July 31, teams can put any player on the waiver wire. If no other teams claim that player, he can be traded to any team. If a team claims a player on waivers, the team that placed the player on waivers has two choices—trade the player to that team or claim him back. The reason for claiming a player is often to block his trade to a rival team. For instance, if your rival needs a left-handed power hitter and one is on the waiver wire, it is probably wise for you to claim him. You don't have to trade for him, and then the other team cannot trade for him.

Occasionally, players slip through the waiver wire and are traded after the deadline. This often happens because the player on the waiver wire is making a lot of money and most teams don't want his salary. Or, teams think that the player will not shift the balance of power enough to cause concern.

# The Beauty of a Pennant Race

## CHAPTER TWELVE

**A *SEASON IS LIKE A LIFETIME.*** It begins with the optimism of youth—when every team has a chance to win the pennant and every player has a chance to have the best year of their careers.

And then the games begin.

One after another, the games are played like days of your life. Sure, this is an overly dramatic way of putting it, yet baseball is a good metaphor for life, and vice versa. And the beauty of baseball is that there are so many games that no single game means more than any other. Yet the games at the end of the year seem to count more because time does indeed run out.

# *The Long Season*

It starts in the spring when the flowers are just beginning to bloom and it ends in the fall when the trees are bare and, in the northern cities at least, there is a bite in the air. A baseball season is long. It develops. Good teams have bad weeks. Bad teams have good weeks. Although consistency is an attribute in baseball, no team or player can go all year on a complete high note. Baseball players and teams go through cycles during the season. That's why baseball is such an interesting sport to watch. Teams take shape over time. There is a dynamic to a baseball season.

Baseball is more of an intellectual game than an emotional one, and for that reason players must stay on an even keel. There will be good games and there will be bad games. This is inevitable in a 162-game marathon of a season, but a player has to guard against getting too high or too low. It is easy to burn out or lose focus either way.

**TIPS**

**TOM'S**

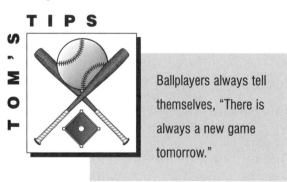

Ballplayers always tell themselves, "There is always a new game tomorrow."

When you get fired up or get down on yourself, you tend to lose focus on what you are doing. If you get too high, you can neglect the things that need to be done, and if you get too low you can start pressing and making your job harder. So baseball players deal with the long season by trying to stay levelheaded and by keeping the season in perspective: all games are important but none are so important that you don't try as hard in others.

Although it is known as a summer game, baseball stretches from the cold days of early April to the cold days of late October. Summer happens in the middle of it.

© Chris Hamilton, Atlanta, GA

Games in June mean something even if they seem to be just part of the long grind. All players know that it can come down to one game at the end of the season. And they know that any game could be the one game that made a difference.

## Pitchers Who "Eat" Innings

The long season is filled with a lot of innings, and each of those innings needs a pitcher. Pitchers who pitch a lot of innings bring great value to their teams. These pitchers are talented and are giving their teams a chance to win. A guy who pitches a lot of innings is considered "a workhorse."

The benchmark for calling a pitcher a workhorse is probably about 200 innings a season. If a pitcher throws 200 innings or more in a season, he is someone a team can rely on game after game to go out there and give his team a legitimate shot at winning.

© Chris Hamilton, Atlanta, GA

**All pitchers know that eating innings is important. I take great pride in the fact that I average about 228 innings a year.**

We all have some games that are better than others. Even a good pitcher will get knocked out early occasionally. But on average, a good pitcher will pitch into the seventh or eighth inning. Of course, not all pitchers who throw a lot of innings win twenty games. Some may only win half of their games. But if a pitcher goes 10-10 for a season, that is still ten wins. And that's something.

Innings-pitched is a significant number for another reason. When a starting pitcher pitches a lot of innings, it means the bullpen gets to rest. A rested bullpen is valuable because it can do the job when it is needed. If a team constantly turns to its bullpen, over time those players will just wear

down. The job description of a starting pitcher is to go in and eat innings and put your team in a position to have a chance to win.

## The Daily Grind

There are injuries in baseball. Players who play every day expend an incredible amount of energy using their legs, backs, arms, knees, and shoulders. Your body consistently takes a pounding because baseball is a game of repetitive movements. You do many of the same things over and over. Some players hold up better than others.

Those who play 150 or more games a year add great value to a team. First, they are good enough for the manager to trust in that position for that many games. Second, they hold up. This is no small thing. If a guy is a great player but he is not playing because he is injured, he doesn't really help the team. Reputation doesn't win games. Players win games. You need your players to play.

Some teams rest players more often than others do, but generally teams want most of their regulars playing together for most of the games. Teams want to put their best players on the field.

## It's Hard Doing It Cal's Way

Consider the accomplishment of Cal Ripken, shortstop and third baseman for the Baltimore Orioles. It is almost impossible for a baseball player to comprehend what he did by playing in 2,632 games in a row. It

is hard for fans to understand the scope of small injuries that happen in the course of a season. Beyond the nagging pains and brief injuries, it seems that every year something really odd happens to somebody.

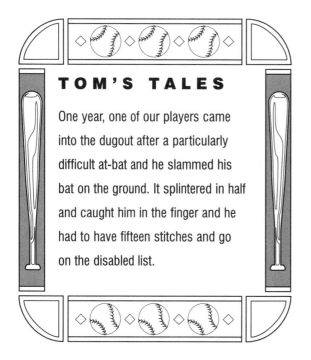

## TOM'S TALES

One year, one of our players came into the dugout after a particularly difficult at-bat and he slammed his bat on the ground. It splintered in half and caught him in the finger and he had to have fifteen stitches and go on the disabled list.

For instance, Dale Murphy tried to catch a ball and ran into the old plywood fence that was in our outfield. His bare hand went up against the wall and the wall separated. When the wall closed it pinched his finger and split it open. It was a crazy weird injury that happens all the time in baseball. Even if you are in great shape, you are going to run into something that will knock you out for a game or two. Cal didn't run into anything for 2,632 games. Amazing.

# *The Importance of a Bench*

In a long season, things happen. Players get hurt or go into slumps or simply need rest. Sometimes key players are traded for someone who does not play their position. In this case, a bench player can become a starter.

If a player replaces an injured starter and the team doesn't miss a beat, he provides incredible stability. These guys are always ready—just in case. Just as a player in the field must know what he will do with the ball if it comes to him, a player on the bench knows that if the opportunity arises he must be ready for it.

## The Birth of the Season

The opening day of baseball season has a mystical nature that seems to inspire poets and artists as well as players and fans. It is a day that changes the order of things. Suddenly, after months of this and that and some other stuff, there is real baseball.

It is another year and once again, these games count.

After the glory and ceremony of opening day, the beginning of a season is a time for adjustment and optimism as each team—no matter the season they had last year or what was written about them in spring training—has a chance to win it all. The records are all the same. Each team has zero

**TIPS**

**TOM'S**

Not all teams that have a high payroll are going to be able to pull things together. It is especially hard for teams with a lot of new players to pull together and become a team. And this is most true at the beginning of a season. Teams have succeeded bringing in many new players, but it has also backfired on teams that find players playing for individual goals and not for a team goal.

wins and zero losses. And then the season begins to settle in—one game at a time, one series at a time.

It is important but not essential to get off to a good start. It is more important for a team that is not expected to do well than it is for a team with a lot of talent. A team with talent generally feels it can right itself before it gets too late. Sometimes, though, it does get too late. But if a team is not expected to do well and gets off to a poor start, this can be a mountain to get past.

## June Gives a Clue

By June, more than fifty games have been played and the season has settled into something of a pattern. Hot streaks and cold streaks have been time tested and teams know what they have and what they need. If somebody is having a good year by June, they are probably going to have a good year. Although things can turn around, they often don't.

## The All-Star Break and the Trading Deadline

By the time you get to the All-Star break in July, you have about half a season behind you. You may be trying to put things back together so you can have a second-half run. Or maybe you are happy where you are and want to try to sustain your lead and maybe even build it.

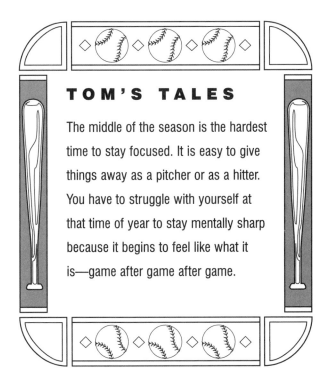

**TOM'S TALES**

The middle of the season is the hardest time to stay focused. It is easy to give things away as a pitcher or as a hitter. You have to struggle with yourself at that time of year to stay mentally sharp because it begins to feel like what it is—game after game after game.

At the end of July the trading deadline rolls around and your team has one final chance to make a move without any opposition (more on the trading deadline in Chapter 11). By then, you know what kind of team you have. If you have an eye on the playoffs and the World Series, you begin to think about some piece that is missing. No matter how good your team is, you know that it can be better. That's the nature of baseball and that is one reason why trades are made mid-season. Teams think they can trade young players with potential to teams that are essentially out of the race. In return, the team in contention gets back a seasoned major league player—maybe a star—who can contribute right now.

# *The Dog Days*

In late July and throughout August, deep summer and deep baseball merge into what are referred to universally in the baseball world as *the dog days*.

In the heart of the summer, baseball can be a tough job even though it is always fun. Hey, hot is hot.

© Chris Hamilton, Atlanta, GA

It's just hotter than a dog. You feel like sitting on a porch and panting, or sipping water and listening to an old man play a banjo. But you play baseball. You walk out of the dugout and feel like you're getting hit by a ton of bricks. It drains you. You go through dead periods at this time when you can't get your body to do what it should, but you force yourself to keep playing. In some stadiums the temperature on the field exceeds 100 degrees. Day after day, it burns into you and just wears down your body. And then the next day you play another game. And then the next day...

# *Watching the Scoreboard in September*

In the end, either you are in the tournament or you watch. The cliché is that you go golfing, but no matter what you do you simply burn because you are not there.

If you have a shot in September, you suddenly find yourself playing games that mean something right now. The time to recover from bad streaks is gone. These games count, one by one, and all you have to do is pick up the newspaper to see where you stand. And if you want to know how things are changing while you play, you can always look up at the scoreboard and see how your rivals are doing in *their* game.

**T I P S**

**T O M ' S**

A team that is not in contention in September has a different dynamic than one that is in contention. A team that is not in contention has players who are playing more for themselves and their careers. They know the team they are on is going to change quite a bit in the off season so they are simply trying to make an impression—either on the management of this team or on that of other teams.

During the last month of the season, teams are allowed to expand their rosters and bring in extra players from the minor leagues. Almost all

teams bring up two to five guys who had great years in the minors and are maybe getting their first or second look at the big leagues. These guys, even on a bad team, bring energy because they are experiencing the dream of major league baseball for the first time. They are so excited and in awe of everything that all players can't help but remember how they felt when they were in a similar position.

September is about figuring out if you have a chance. Even if you are on a team that is assured of making the playoffs early on, as we were in 1998, you still watch the scoreboard to see who you might be playing. I still watch to see if the Red Sox won, and I imagine many players check on their original hometown team. Players watch because we are fans too, and we want to see who is winning, even in the other league. It is interesting. But in 1998, the biggest story in scoreboard watching was whether Mark McGwire or Sammy Sosa hit another home run.

# The Playoffs and the World Series

## CHAPTER THIRTEEN

**THE FANTASY IS THE SAME** from the time ballplayers first put on a glove or pick up a bat. I had it as a kid in little league and it's the same for me now playing in the big leagues, even after accomplishing the goal once. In fact, I probably want it even more now. It's the same for all players because there is only one legitimate baseball fantasy—winning the World Series.

In the end, that's why we play the game.

Individual goals and accomplishments are great, and all players need to put up good enough numbers to survive in major league baseball. We all dream of big numbers and awards, and in our wildest fantasies we dream of getting inducted into the Hall Of Fame. But we play baseball because we want to know what it's like to win the World Series. I've already won one. I want to know what it's like to win another. And if I win another, I'll

want to know about winning a third. I am a professional baseball player. I dream of championships.

Getting to the World Series is excruciating, gut wrenching, intense—and fun. Playing in it is even better.

And my team won it once. It's what I think about every day. I want it again.

## Who Makes the Playoffs?

The four teams that make the playoffs in each league are the champions of each of the three divisions and the wild card team.

In the first round of the playoffs, the Wild Card round, the team with the best record in the league plays against the wild card team. The other two division champions play against each other.

**TIPS**

**TOM'S**

I think it is easier for a less talented team to win a five-game series against a more talented team than it is to win a seven-game series. A team can get lucky and sneak off a couple of wins and then it is only one win away from winning a five-game series. But it's a bit tougher to sneak off four wins. Over time talent shows through more.

In this round, the team with the best regular season record gets home field advantage. This means that in a five-game series, that team will play three of the games in its home stadium. The first two games are played in its home stadium, and if there is a fifth game it will also be played in that team's home stadium. The third and fourth games are played in their opponent's home stadium.

The next round is the League Championship Series, which, like the World Series, lasts seven games. The first two games and the last two games of this seven-game series are played in the park of the team with home field advantage.

In the World Series, home field advantage switches back and forth between leagues in alternating years. If the American League has it one year, the National League has it the next.

## The Dynamics of a Five-Game Series

Clearly every game in the playoffs is important, but I think that the first game of a five-game series has added weight and significance. This is because one team only has to win three games.

If you lose Game 1, the other team only needs two more victories to send you home. And you still need three. If you win the first game, it gives you a huge psychological boost because you only need two more wins. Of course, the importance of that game is even greater if you are playing at home. If you lose Game 1 at home, you have not only dug yourself into a hole but you have also lost home field advantage; because if the other team wins its two games at home it wins the series.

If you lose Game 1 in the other team's ballpark, it is not such a disaster because the other team is "supposed to" win at home. All you have to do when you visit is win one of the first two games, because then you will have home field advantage.

And, as important as Game 1 is, subsequent games are more important. It's the rule of the playoffs. Intensity goes up each step of the way.

If you win the first two games, you have a huge advantage no matter where the next games are played because you only have to win one more game. The other team has to sweep three straight games and that's difficult to do in the regular season and almost impossible in the playoffs. But from time to time it happens.

### Setting Your Pitching Rotation

Although teams use a five-man rotation in the regular season, in a five-game series most teams use only three starting pitchers. Teams let their top two pitchers pitch in the first two games and the last two games.

# The Dynamics of a Seven-Game Series

Although it seems simple, winning one extra game in a seven-game play-off series is significantly harder than winning a five-game series.

The first game in a seven-game series is not as important to either team as the first game in a five-game series. There is a little bit of time to

recover in a seven-game series. It's desperate but not so desperate as to cause panic.

Since the first two games are played in the city of the team with the best regular season record, the visiting team wants to get a split. Win one and lose one and the team is happy. The team with home field advantage wants to keep the advantage. So it feels more pressure to win those first two games. Then it can go to the other team's ballpark for three straight games and not worry about elimination. If you split two games at home, you may not make it back home again to play in front of your fans.

As the series progresses your emotions change. If, for instance, you go down 2-0, you suddenly find you are in a heap of trouble. But if you are up 2-0 you know that one more win starts to put a nail in the coffin of your opponent's season. If the series is tied 1-1, both teams still have a chance at winning.

If after three games you are up 3-0, you can almost taste the championship. But that's the time to attack and work even harder. Otherwise, if you are down 3-0 you are on the brink of watching your dream disappear. That's tough and desperate.

## Setting Your Pitching Rotation

In a seven-game series, all the games are of utmost importance. In the old days, teams used three starting pitchers and expected their ace pitcher to pitch games 1, 4, and 7. Some teams still do it that way, but others use four starting pitchers so the top three pitchers pitch the first three games and

the last three games. The fourth starter only pitches the fourth game. The reason for this strategy is to give the three best pitchers an extra day of rest. And rest makes a difference for a pitcher.

## *Players React to the Crowd*

Players can hear. The crowd and home field absolutely do make a difference to a team. It's not a huge difference because ballplayers are professionals trained not to react too emotionally to the ups and downs of a long season. We know that there will be cheers and even some boos. We can hear.

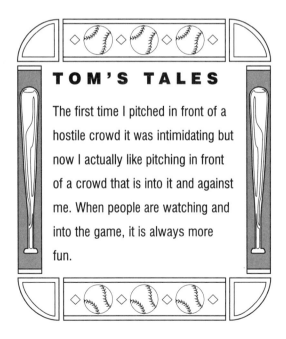

**TOM'S TALES**

The first time I pitched in front of a hostile crowd it was intimidating but now I actually like pitching in front of a crowd that is into it and against me. When people are watching and into the game, it is always more fun.

Baseball players have emotions. Playing at home, the crowd is cheering for you and you can feed off of their electricity. It's real. When the home field crowd is loud and emotional, your adrenaline starts to pump. When you are on the road and 50,000 people scream in unison against you, it can also get your adrenaline pumping and press you to "show them." Usually when your adrenaline is pumping you have more energy—physical and emotional—and you perform better. But sometimes it can backfire. For me, if I take that energy and try to force myself to throw a 100 mph fastball past a batter, it isn't going to work.

## *The Intensity Level Keeps Increasing*

From the playoffs to the World Series the pressure and intensity increase round by round, game by game, and inning by inning. The 162-game marathon is over. This is the sprint to the finish line of the post season.

© Chris Hamilton, Atlanta, GA

**In the playoffs, the tension continues to go up because more is at stake.**

The first round of five games is perhaps most difficult to deal with because you realize that even if you had a tremendous season it can all disappear in three games. Three wins. That's all it takes. It is especially tough if you are the better team and you lose. You are supposed to win that series. It is just a bump in the road—a bump that disables the entire motorcade of supposed destiny.

A longer series tests a team's ability to sustain momentum. There is a little less luck involved. That one extra game necessary to advance makes a difference. The League Championship Series is tough because you know you are one step away from a chance to play in the World Series.

Although winning the World Series is always the only and ultimate goal, teams often feel relieved just getting to the World Series, because that is something much more than merely making the playoffs.

## *The Joy and Pressure of the World Series*

Two teams show up for Christmas. One team gets a brand new bicycle. The other gets a lump of coal. That's the World Series. Only later does the losing team realize that the lump of coal is still okay because no one else in the neighborhood even got to see Santa Claus. But at the time, the emotions are of winning and losing—as opposite as can be.

I have been in the World Series and won once, and I have lost more than once. It is always fun to play, yet gut-wrenching because it shakes you to the core. That is the beauty of it. It is so much fun.

There are a lot of distractions if you play in the World Series, but players have to keep their attention on the job at hand—to play baseball games. A championship is at stake. *I want the bicycle for Christmas, not the lump of coal.*

Baseball players play baseball because the competition is so enticing. Somebody wins and somebody loses. It all comes down to the World Series—dramatic, climactic, emotional, and visual—like Hollywood and Broadway combined with prime time television.

The beginning of the World Series is the beginning of a story with an unwritten ending. This story has a six-month prologue. And that is the beauty of the World Series: the season is the prologue. When there is a great World Series it becomes the story of that year, the story that is told for generations. Even if the World Series is a blowout, the team that wins is automatically attached to that year.

## Playing in a World Series

The two teams that play in a World Series don't really know each other in the same way that teams from the same league know each other. Plus, both teams play with or without the designated hitter during part of the Series. It's just different.

Scouting reports inform teams that certain players do something well and have trouble with something else. If you are a pitcher, you learn what types of pitches cause each player trouble. Then, if you are a smart pitcher, you mostly ignore the scouting reports.

I am convinced that players often get into trouble in the World Series by listening to scouting reports rather than simply trusting what they do best. A pitcher can get into a lot of trouble by trying to pitch to a hitter's weakness instead of pitching their best strategy. For instance, if I am facing a hitter who is best at hitting the outside pitch, I am still going to throw it to him because that is what I do best. If that is what he hits best and that is what I throw best, my attitude is, *Here, I dare you.* If he beats me, then I'll make an adjustment and exercise a new strategy. Until then, we both know what's happening.

In a World Series where the pitcher and batter are unfamiliar with each other, I would guess that the pitcher has an advantage. The batter can study videotape but he still won't really know what a pitcher's best pitch is.

## *Winning and Losing the World Series*

The World Series only offers two alternatives —

- Top of the mountain
- Bottom of the valley

Remember, the season starts in February during spring training, where more players participate than the 750 that ultimately fill the rosters. Each team invites between forty and seventy players to spring training. Then, more than six months later, there are fifty players left.

Two teams. Top of the mountain or bottom of the valley.

It is the gift you've been asking for since February that only one of two teams gets. As you contemplate the outcome of the World Series as a member of one of those two teams, you either feel the greatest elation possible or the most incredible regret that a person can experience in sports.

In the end,
only one team wins.

© Chris Hamilton, Atlanta, GA

Winning is obvious. *Yes!* And then it takes weeks to sink in. You have dreamt of this championship win your entire life and yet it is even more than you imagined. It is something that millions have dreamt of at one time or another.

Losing burns. Suddenly the dream disappears and an empty feeling remains—a sort of bitterness. You can only think about how incredibly

close you were to the *ultimate accomplishment* only to see it disappear. The circumstances matter and yet they don't matter. You lost. What else matters? After a few weeks you realize that the season wasn't a waste. You played in the World Series—the World Series! Sure, losing hurts. But yet up until then... wow!

# The Business of the Game

## CHAPTER FOURTEEN

**SHOES. CARS, SODA, BEER, AND CREDIT CARDS. STORES.**

Stuff.

Baseball sells stuff, even tickets. Baseball sells luxury boxes, concessions, parking, and television rights. That's how baseball makes money directly because, in 90s terminology, baseball is "great content."

On television, in stadiums, in publications, on the Internet, baseball is entertainment and it sells. Baseball is such "great content" because almost everybody loves to watch baseball. The attraction is evident in the publication of this book, in the presentation of all the baseball shows on television, in literary musings of many great American men and women of letters. It is evident in the face of a child wearing a hometown hat—a young consumer who already loves the product.

Baseball is an easy sell. Even after all the labor troubles of 1994, which somewhat damaged the reputations of players and owners, the game continues to thrive. Baseball's drama and athleticism appeal to the competitive soul of the richest country in the world. We've all played. It connects us.

Baseball sells stuff, a lot of stuff, and baseball makes money, a lot of money. Therefore, it is a business.

## *Why Money Matters*

Baseball has a lot of money. Therefore, it gets a lot of attention. Money matters in major league baseball because money matters everywhere, and the more you have the more you can afford to get. Money matters because some teams have more of it than others and can afford to bid on more stars.

The playing field is not completely level—at least in terms of team payrolls. Some teams have a much higher payroll than others and that often translates into more talent and ultimately more wins. But, it doesn't always work out that way. Sometimes teams picked to finish in last place go to the World Series. It happens. I know because it happened to a team I was on early in my career. I also know that teams expected to win often do win. That has happened to me in my career as well. And I have been on great teams that have not won it all.

I know that money matters because it attracts talent. But I know that real victories are always won by the players, not the accountants.

## Time Is Money

Players make a lot of money if they play for many years in the major leagues. Time of service is important. A player can't really make a lot of money during the first few years in the major leagues because he doesn't have the freedom to negotiate with any team except the one he belongs to. He is property. It takes time to earn the right to be a free agent.

Along the way, he earns other rights.

## Starting Out

It must be this way for every player: *I can't believe they are going to pay me (the minimum salary—for me it was $62,500) to play baseball.* I remember playing in the minor leagues making $1,000 per month and thinking how great it would be to make the minimum—more than my dad ever made in any one year—and I was only twenty-one years old. It was a lot of money then, and the minimum now—$175,000—is still a lot of money to the rest of the world. But in the world of professional athletics—which is, after all, the world of show business—it is not exactly breaking the bank.

When you first enter the major leagues, you understand that some players make a lot more money than you. At the time, it doesn't matter. Even if you outperform others, you are so happy to be where you are that you just look at the older players and think that you will soon be there. If you perform, you *will* soon be there. If not, you will soon be gone—back to the minors for more development.

## *The First Three Years*

A player belongs to his team in the first three years and he must accept the contract offered for each of those years. There is no room to negotiate. A player can have a tremendous year—hitting fifty home runs or winning twenty-two games—and it doesn't matter. The team only has to pay him the minimum major league salary—currently $175,000.

The interesting dynamic in this process is that the young player remembers how he is treated. In the future, if he lasts and performs, he will have bargaining power.

## *Arbitration*

At three years, the player begins to get some rights. After three years of service a player is allowed to file for arbitration. This happens when the player and the team cannot reach an agreement on a salary, so they go to an arbitrator. Each side presents a number and an argument as to why that is the fairest figure, and then the arbitrator chooses one of the two numbers. That number becomes the player's salary for the year. The player's job is to make as much money as he can and the team's job is to save as much money as it can.

Players have to understand that the process involves criticism. The player must decide if he is willing to hear this for more money. Of course, it also depends on how much money is involved.

### HOW IT WORKS

There is a select group of guys who are eligible
for arbitration before three years of service time.
They are called the "Super Twos." The easiest
explanation is that all of them have more than two years
and less than three years of service. The top 10 percent
(in terms of service time) of these players are allowed
to file for arbitration. Of all the players who have played
between two and three years, those who have been in the
big leagues for the longest time are eligible for arbitration.

For both sides, the negotiation is always in comparison to something.
Comparisons are made to players with a little more service time.
Comparing yourself to an eleven-year veteran wouldn't be helpful.

When a player has played for three years, he has a record, and he compares that record as favorably as he can to players who make as much or
more money. The idea is to try to find a slot. Owners can find lower-salaried players for comparison.

When a player files a number and a team files a number, the arbitrator
can only choose one of these numbers. He cannot choose a number in
between the two. The midpoint is the breaking point of arbitration.

If a team thinks a player is worth $1 million a year and the player
thinks he is worth $4 million a year, that's a big gap. And the midpoint
is $2.5 million. The player has to prove he is worth one penny more than

$2.5 million to be awarded his contract. On the other hand, if the player had filed at $3 million, the midpoint would be $2 million. That is an easier number to prove. Of course, this works both ways. If the team offers a little more money, it pushes the midpoint up.

**TOM'S TIPS**

Usually the argument is something like, *Hey, I put up numbers as good as or better than (name a player) and he is making (name an amount) more than me. I deserve as much as him.*

One goal of arbitration is for arbitration to be avoided. Since it is in the interest of both sides to compromise, hopefully both sides will recognize the wisdom of negotiating to agree on a salary.

## Stories of Arbitration

Some players get through arbitration just fine and don't take the process personally. Others are offended by the way it works. Just as players try to build themselves up, a team puts them down in an effort to save money.

The hard part for players to understand is that it is the team's job to talk you down so that they don't have to pay you the extra money. Some arbitrations are like courtroom battles.

I remember when I was in the minors I heard the story of one prominent player who had finished two All-Star years in a row. He came out of arbitration wondering how he ever got to the big leagues. They ripped him up. After something like that, it doesn't matter to the player if he wins or loses. He remembers overemphasized flaws and that his abilities and accomplishments were minimized or trivialized. A lot of guys who have gone to arbitration have come back bitter about what happened.

In the end, after the hearing, a decision is made that day. And that is it. But sometimes, bad feelings linger on long enough for the player to file for free agency. If it reaches that point, the player will often leave rather than negotiate with the team.

Sometimes an agreement is made between a player and his team just before the arbitration hearing is scheduled to start.

The end of the arbitration process often depends on the personality of the player. Obviously, just like anything in life, it is better if two people agree than if one person wins and one loses.

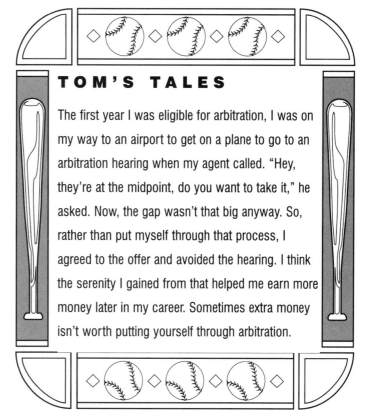

### TOM'S TALES

The first year I was eligible for arbitration, I was on my way to an airport to get on a plane to go to an arbitration hearing when my agent called. "Hey, they're at the midpoint, do you want to take it," he asked. Now, the gap wasn't that big anyway. So, rather than put myself through that process, I agreed to the offer and avoided the hearing. I think the serenity I gained from that helped me earn more money later in my career. Sometimes extra money isn't worth putting yourself through arbitration.

## Why Teams and Young Players Agree to Long Contracts

There are certain players who are obviously going to be stars unless something unforeseen happens. Of course, in baseball weird things happen all the time, and young players become stars all the time too.

In the 1990s, a new trend is that teams sign their young players to long-term contracts.

When it is clear to a team that it has a young player who is going to be a star for a long time, it is in the interest of that team to sign that player to a long-term contract. They should sign him before he is eligible for arbitration and before he is eligible to be a free agent. When a team does not have to give a player money, but does, it hopes that the player will stay beyond the arbitration stage without conflict. The team treats a player well now and hopes the player will treat the team well later.

A long contract gives the player the advantage of security. When a young player is given millions of dollars he knows that no matter what he does he will be okay. It is much easier to relax and concentrate on baseball.

The key for a team is to figure out which guys will use this feeling to their advantage. There are players who take comfort in the loyalty given to them and others who will take advantage of a lot of money early on. Good teams recognize the difference because money is a key ingredient of success. Yet most players always give their all. Maybe 1 percent think about their contract when they are on the field. Of course, as the saying goes, one bad apple spoils the bunch. So the reputation of greed persists.

But fans and players think about the same thing—winning, and that's all that counts in the record books.

# Non-Glamour Free Agents and Trades

Superstars get all the attention, and yet every year a lot of players are simply released by their teams. This does not mean they are undesirable players. It simply means that teams have decided not to bid on them. And thus, they are free.

The superstars get all the attention, but it is the players who are released or traded who move the most. Although everybody makes a lot of money, not everybody plays where they want to play.

# Free Agents

Baseball is a game of capitalism. The greatest players (who have most recently negotiated a contract) make the most money.

When a player becomes a free agent, he is facing the opportunity of a lifetime. If he has had success in his career, he will find that many teams are interested in his talents. And that is flattering.

And so there must be a decision. Ideally, a player wants to go to a team that has the greatest chance to win *and* that offers him the most money. That doesn't always happen.

## *Making Decisions*

Money counts for a lot. That's all there is to say on that. Money counts. This is America and that's one of the ways we keep score.

Money is not all that counts for baseball players because plenty have not gone for every last penny. It depends on the situation.

## *The Hometown Discount*

The list of players who chose to go for *more* than money begins at the beginning of the A's and goes all the way to the Z's—pausing in the G's to at least list *Glavine*. That's right, I did not go for every last penny when I negotiated my last contract. In fact, I settled my contract before I was able to become a free agent. I did not test the waters. I wanted to stay in the comfort of Atlanta. Easy for me to say, I suppose, since I *settled* for a little money that is a *lot* more than most people will ever make.

I know. I play baseball. But I also know my worth. I could have earned more money if I pursued other options. I chose Atlanta. It turned out great. I think Atlanta is happy, too.

## *Money, Players, TV—What Does It All Mean?*

In the end, players win games, and teams that win games make money. The teams give some of this money to the players. It seems so simple and circular.

Teams in big cities get more money from local television than teams in small cities. This can make a huge difference in revenue and thus a huge difference in the amount of money teams can pay to good players. So some teams spend more than others because they have more to spend. In many ways this is not totally unfair because business practices should come into play. Yet a team is something of a public trust. Getting a team to click on all cylinders takes enormous effort. A half-hearted effort will never work in any endeavor, and certainly not in professional baseball.

But money makes it a lot easier for talented people to work together because sometimes it is the only way to get these talented people together.

# The Minor Leagues

## CHAPTER FIFTEEN

**THE PURPOSE OF THE MINOR LEAGUES** is to get a young player into a system of playing ball. A young player—from high school or college or another country—is a raw talent. A major league team drafts about seventy players a year and brings in many others from outside the United States. All of these players are funneled into a big minor league system that narrows until the twenty-five best players in each organization fill out the roster of the big league club.

Along the way, there are different levels. The newest players start at the lowest level. After that, they rise according to their talent and accomplishments. The ultimate goal in the minor leagues is to develop well-rounded major league baseball players.

## Why Players Need to be Developed and How This Is Done

A team has to have a philosophy that can be translated into action in order to be successful. For instance, having a player field 100 ground balls a day doesn't translate into a philosophy. But if the idea is for that player to field each ground ball using the proper fundamental form and working on all the mechanics to make it right for him, that is a strong philosophy of "do it right." That stuff sticks with a player and it makes a player learn along the way—even when things go wrong.

A team also has to look at its organization with a wide lens. For instance, the Braves have pitchers John Smoltz, Greg Maddux, and myself signed for the next few years, but we are all in our thirties. So the Braves probably want to start developing some young pitchers. The idea is to always feed new talent into your major league club. You do it by drafting a number of players at a certain position and working with them, hoping some of them pan out.

## The Draft

Teams pick seventy new players each year, plus they get free agent players. All of these players are added to the mix of players already in the organization. Most will not make it to the minors. Thus many players are drafted because predicting the future abilities of young baseball players is a very inexact science.

Although top draft picks get a lot of publicity and money in the beginning, there are plenty of stars selected in the lower rounds. Some players hit the peak of their baseball abilities at eighteen. These players may be high draft picks because they are expected to advance.

The job of the scout is to predict the future. This is a tough job because many different kinds of players become good baseball players, thus many very similar players never make it.

## HOW IT WORKS

Scouts can think a player will turn out to be good and he won't develop. Or scouts will be pleasantly surprised when a 5'10" 160-pound guy develops in two years into a 6'3" 230-pound fireballer. Young men fill out and it is the scout's job to try to predict it.

Plus, scouts try to figure out players' personalities. There is just no way to really know a guy's heart and determination. You just have to watch. Psychological tests help teams determine what makes a player tick. But I think the true test is still on the field. You might have a guy who is a physical monster with an overpowering fastball, but he could turn to mush the first time he faces trouble on the field. There are other guys who buckle down and get down to business when they run into trouble.

Talent versus will is always a question, and I would always choose to go with the player who tries a little bit harder even if he doesn't have as much talent as another player. I would never want a player on my team who is going to quit when things go bad.

## High Draft Picks

High draft picks are under a lot of pressure because they make more money than most players, and some of these "bonus babies" can't handle it. Jealousy and backstabbing are involved in the minor leagues, so smart players pick their friends carefully and hang around with other players not concerned with money.

I was a second round draft pick. I know that there are plenty of second round draft picks who fail and yet I also know that the status of where I was drafted gave me an advantage. In professional baseball you are compensated based on where you were drafted. When a team invests in a player, it wants that player to succeed. So a high draft pick is given every chance imaginable to succeed because there is a lot invested in him.

About a half-million dollars is invested in a kid from the time he enters the minors until the time he gets to the big leagues. That's about the average. For some kids it is less; for some, it is a lot more; and many don't make it at all.

# The Difference Between College and the Minors

In some ways, college ball is similar to minor league ball because both have a high concentration of players in their late teens and early twenties. But the differences between the two are profound.

The goal in college baseball is to win.

The goal in the minor leagues is to develop major league baseball players. This is the advantage teams have when that player has been in the minor leagues for four years. After four years in the minors, you don't have to undo what a college coach did or did not teach him. You don't have to worry that the player was in a system in which wins were more important than player development.

In the minors, a player can have a successful season simply because he improved. Even if he didn't put up the best numbers or if a pitcher didn't win as many games as you would like, he can still be considered successful. If he showed progress from the start of the season to the end, there is a good chance his organization will keep him and move him up to the next level. The emphasis is on development more than production.

# Rookie League

The beginning of professional baseball is rookie league—where players from all over come together with one common goal. Teams usually have more than one rookie league team in more than one league, and these teams have first-year draftees and players from other countries. Players in

rookie league ball come from so many different backgrounds that every player suffers some kind of culture shock. Some players become your friends, others don't, but you respect all of them on the field.

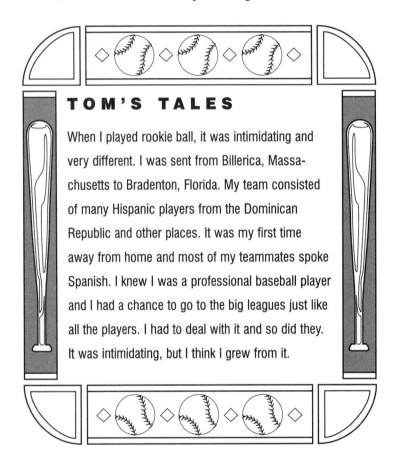

### TOM'S TALES

When I played rookie ball, it was intimidating and very different. I was sent from Billerica, Massachusetts to Bradenton, Florida. My team consisted of many Hispanic players from the Dominican Republic and other places. It was my first time away from home and most of my teammates spoke Spanish. I knew I was a professional baseball player and I had a chance to go to the big leagues just like all the players. I had to deal with it and so did they. It was intimidating, but I think I grew from it.

There were about thirty guys on my rookie team and the talent levels were vastly different. You could tell who had a chance to go somewhere and you knew which players were just there to fill roster spots. It was interesting because often the guys who thought they were on their way really weren't, and others who were not highly regarded were able to rise up. That's how baseball works.

Yet, usually you can pick out the high draft picks. Talent stands out and everybody can see it.

# Getting Cut

It happens by mail. After rookie ball, either you get a contract that offers you a place for the next season or you get a pink slip that tells you you have been released.

The next year, some players will get cut during spring training and that is the end of the line.

# A Ball

After rookie ball comes A ball, which has two levels—high A and low A.

- **High A**—Full of guys who have some college experience and some other guys who are more talented.

- **Low A**—Full of the rawest of the raw. These are young players who are just starting in professional baseball.

At this level the point is to learn. Mostly, ball clubs try to teach young players the fundamentals. It is important for young players to learn to play the game smartly and correctly. Ball clubs hope that some players at this level will blossom into major league ballplayers. They just don't know which ones.

## *AA Ball*

This level is full of the brightest untested young talent. In recent years, many players have jumped from AA ball all the way to the majors. AA ballplayers are often very talented—many future superstars are beginning to make names for themselves.

## *AAA Ball*

AAA ball resembles big league baseball. Stadiums are bigger and players travel by airplane, not by bus. Talented young players are fine tuning their skills before they reach the majors, and major league players sent back to the AAA are trying to make their way back up.

## *Always Learning*

Ballplayers are always learning, even after they leave the minor leagues. The fundamentals always need work. There is no such thing as a perfect ballplayer and all of us know that. There is often a fine line between success and failure.

Players can learn from older players. If another guy has been in a certain situation before, you can pick his brain about what he thinks is the proper way to handle it. Even if the player is wrong it is always worth listening. Hey, advice is free. The more information you have the easier it is to make the right decisions. You have to be smart enough to listen to advice and smart enough to know what works for you.

It helps to try things. If an older player offers a younger player some advice on how to do something, it never hurts to give it a shot. Somebody might show you a new way to throw a curve or a slider. You might say to yourself that it isn't going to work, or you might try it and it does work. After a few attempts you might begin to feel you can do it that way. It doesn't always work, but advice is always free.

The best teacher is experience. Once you go out there and think, *Hey, I've been in this situation before*, it is much easier to stay calm. If you know what to expect, you know what to do.

## Money in the Minors and Two-Way Contracts

As you go up in the minors, you make more money, but it isn't much. When I was in rookie ball, I made $700 a month. In A ball I made $800 a month, in AA ball I made $1,000 a month, and in AAA ball I made $1,500 a month. Ballplayers are in the minors because they love to play baseball, not for the money. You get the money when you get to the majors.

Some experienced AAA players have two-way contracts. They receive a certain amount of money to play in the minors and a minimum major league salary when they play in the major leagues.

## Traveling without Planes

Buses are a grind. Players pay their dues sitting on buses watching the miles go by. In the minors, especially AA, you ride buses everywhere—for

as long as fifteen or twenty hours. You leave at midnight and get in at two in the afternoon the next day and then you have a game that night. It is far from glamorous.

In AAA, you fly in the middle of the night and often have layovers, so you sit in an airport terminal at 4 A.M. waiting to catch a flight. But at least you are flying.

Traveling in the major leagues is entirely different. The difference between the minors and the major leagues is the difference between one-star treatment and five-star treatment.

## *Making the Leap to the Show*

The leap to the major leagues is a huge leap and it is quite an accomplishment just to make it there. That's when guys get in trouble. Players are so relieved when they finally make it that they relax a bit.

There is a difference between "Getting There" and "Staying There." The cliché that it is easier to get to the big leagues than it is to stay is true. The good life of the major leagues is enticing, and if a player doesn't discipline himself to work even harder once he gets there, he may only stay for a short time.

Players talk about those who "made it to the Show for a cup of coffee." This means they stuck around for only a short time and then they were back in the minors. If it happens, it can be a slap in the face because a lot of guys never get a second chance. The ones lucky enough to get a second chance are more serious and focused the next time.

Teams can help a player get through early difficulties. I know the Braves certainly helped me when I lost seventeen games my first year. Although I lost so much, I was still learning more than I ever could have by winning seventeen in AAA ball. The fact that the Braves kept putting me out on the mound despite my record told me a lot about how they felt. They believed in me and that meant a lot in those early frustrating times. They helped me deal with adversity and they made me a stronger player.

My turning point came the following year when I knew I did not have to fight for a roster spot. My confidence was up because I was mentally strong enough to handle most anything, and because of what I learned from the Braves that first year.

# The Art of Pitching

PART FIVE

**THIS PART OF THE BOOK WAS THE MOST FUN TO WRITE.** I am what I am—a pitcher. Here I cover the different jobs of different pitchers and then I explain specifically how to throw various pitches. Finally, I address the most important aspect of pitching, the mental aspect. The battle between a pitcher and a batter is a war of skill, nerves, strategy, and cunning.

# Starters and Relievers, Lefties and Righties

## CHAPTER SIXTEEN

**PITCHING IS THE MOST IMPORTANT ELEMENT OF THE GAME OF BASEBALL.**
In any given game a pitcher runs the show, but a pitcher is not like a
quarterback in football. In a season you need more than one pitcher to be
successful and just to compete. One pitcher cannot pitch every inning of
every game. More likely, a starting pitcher will pitch some innings in 20
percent of a team's games. And a relief pitcher, though pitching in more
games, will pitch fewer innings.

Each team needs ten or eleven pitchers. Five are starting pitchers, and the
rest are relief pitchers. In theory, at least one of the starting pitchers and
two of the relief pitchers are left-handed. This is not always true for starting pitchers, since it is difficult to find left-handed starters. But every team
has a couple of left-handed relief pitchers.

# *Finding and Using Five Starters*

The long season subjects a lot of arms to wear and tear. Good teams find five pitchers they can rely on week after week. Other teams spend a whole season testing them, trying to find five they can depend on.

In the best scenario, a team would have two good left-handed starters. Unfortunately, there are not a lot of left-handed starters. The thirty major league baseball teams each have an average of ten or eleven pitchers. Of those pitchers, about 25 percent are left-handed.

Beyond the arm pitchers throw with, teams would like to have:

   #1 Pitcher—a star; potential best pitcher in baseball

   #2 Pitcher—a winning pitcher, an inning eater;
               the potential #1 Pitcher

   #3 Pitcher—an inning eater; a winner capable of a great year

   #4 Pitcher—an inning eater who wins his share

   #5 Pitcher—an inning eater or a young guy with huge potential

Since no two pitchers are exactly alike, it is difficult to accurately describe a typical pitching staff. On the Atlanta Braves' talented pitching staff, for example, our #1, #2 and #3 starters have won Cy Young Awards. Other teams struggle to find any consistent pitchers.

# *Why Teams Want a Lefty*

I am a left-handed pitcher and this is an advantage because, all through little league, high school, and the minors, batters just don't face many lefties. So when they do, batters have to make an adjustment.

**It is good to be a left-handed pitcher.**

© Chris Hamilton, Atlanta, GA

**TOM'S TIPS**

Teams would rather have an adequate left-hander than an adequate right-hander because left-handers are harder to find. There's just not that many of them. And, there are so many right-handers available that teams probably don't have to settle for an adequate one.

In life and especially in baseball, the more you see something the more you are ready for it. And batters see a lot of right-handed pitchers. That's just the way humans are—mostly right-handed.

When the ball is thrown by a lefty, it is speeding toward the batter on a different and less-familiar plane. As the batter prepares, it's like looking at a right-handed pitcher in the mirror—everything is backward.

For instance, a left-handed pitcher facing a right-handed batter throws balls that move away from the batter. But a right-handed pitcher throws balls that generally move toward the batter. It's a different movement altogether.

If a team can mix up its pitching staff up and, let's say, start with a righty today, a lefty tomorrow, and then a righty, a lefty, and a righty—it forces guys who play every day to alter the way they think. And, it forces the manager of the other team to platoon the guys who don't play every day. A mix of pitchers forces the other team to make day-to-day adjustments; getting into a groove hurts them. For instance, they can't think, *Well, for three days in a row we are facing right-handers who throw 95 mph*. And even if they are facing three right-handers with different approaches, it is still easier to make adjustments between right-handers than it is to adjust back and forth between right-handers and left-handers.

## *Pitchers Need Rest*

Teams now use five pitchers in a rotation. A few decades ago, teams used four pitchers. Somewhere along the way, pitchers began to need more rest.

The truth is that we don't really need the rest. By the fourth day, most of us are ready to pitch. But the extra day helps, and teams have recognized this. In addition, teams now invest a lot of money in pitchers, so they do everything they can to take care of them.

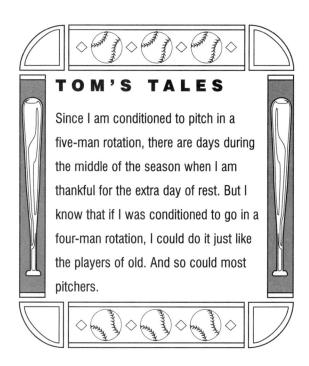

## TOM'S TALES

Since I am conditioned to pitch in a five-man rotation, there are days during the middle of the season when I am thankful for the extra day of rest. But I know that if I was conditioned to go in a four-man rotation, I could do it just like the players of old. And so could most pitchers.

## *How Can a Pitcher Be Too Strong?*

If it rains or there is an off-day, pitchers get extra rest. If a pitcher doesn't pitch when he is supposed to, he can lose his touch and lose control of his pitches. He overthrows everything because his muscles had the chance to get a little stronger, so he suddenly throws harder and with less touch than

he wants. He is not used to this much power, which causes his ball to go all over the place.

### The Post Season: Less Rest Necessary

Most teams go to a three-man rotation in the playoffs. If a team—such as ours in 1998—has four great starters, it will try to use them because that gives everybody an extra day of rest. But when it comes down to the sudden-death format of the playoffs, pitchers aren't really resting up. Sure, pitchers need some rest. But pressure and adrenaline keep them going. The aches seem to ache less because you really don't think about them. When playing baseball at its highest level, who needs rest?

# The Evolution

In the old days, pitchers worked more. Starting pitchers pitched in four-man rotations further into a game. The game has become more and more specialized over the past thirty or so years.

It is not better or worse, it's just different, significantly different. Not long ago starting pitchers pitched with less rest and relievers were brought in only when the pitcher on the mound was in trouble.

But this is the age of the specialist. Specialization has developed because managers are looking for certain players to do certain things. It works.

One of the first relief specialists was Rollie Fingers, who was devastating for the Oakland A's teams of the 1970s. Here he is when he played for the Milwaukee Brewers.

© Steve Babineau

The first specialist was the *closer*, the guy who comes in and finishes off a game that his team is winning. Closers used to come into the game in the seventh, eighth, or ninth inning, whenever the team felt it was in danger and had a chance to close out the game. Inevitably, this guy would come into a dangerous situation with men on base and the game on the line. He was expected to pitch outs and to get you out of a jam.

But the closer's role has changed along with the roles of all the players in the bullpen. They are not generalists anymore. Every guy has some sort of specialty.

# Closers

Here is the theory on fireballing closers, who generally come in throwing heat: If you have a pitcher who has been pitching eight innings and is tiring and maybe getting a little slower, it can't hurt to give the other team a change of pace. And if you are going to change the pace, why not with the hardest throwing arm on the team. Maybe he doesn't have the best variety of pitches, so he couldn't go nine innings. But for three outs, a guy with a huge arm can be hard to adjust to if the previous pitcher was slower. If, all of a sudden, at the end of a game, the team is facing a live, fresh arm pitching up to 100 mph, that can be discombobulating.

Teams started trying closers and noticed that they worked. So more teams used them. Often, the closer was brought into the game before the ninth inning, and most times he was brought in with men on base.

Then the thinking changed again. Teams thought, *Hey, this guy can get us out of trouble, so why not bring him in before the trouble even starts.* Thus, the role of closer in recent years has evolved into that of a three-out specialist. He comes in to start (and finish) the final half inning. He comes in at the beginning of a half inning with no one on base. His job is simple—to get three outs.

## In the Mind of a Closer

*These guys have no chance.* That's what a closer is thinking as he approaches the mound. The other team is simply wasting their time even

trying. He's there to throw to three batters and that's all he intends to throw to. *Here, take this!*

Confidence is the greatest weapon for any athlete but it seems magnified in the role of a closer. If a closer believes, he shows it. Confidence is a great thing.

Closers have to be able to shrug off a failure because, inevitably, they will have a bad inning. They have to be able to go right out there again the next day and not worry about the past. Confidence has to overpower any bad experiences, and confidence must be fed with good experiences. Closers often have insecurities and overpower them with self-confidence. If he believes, it shows in his swagger and in his pitching.

## Why Closers Don't Start

Closers have great stuff but they often don't have the stamina to be starters. It's a different job. Closers come in and throw everything possible to get three batters out. A starter has a different job. He has to come in and *work*. His job is to last deep into the game so that no other pitcher is needed. He is not required to overpower or dominate. The game is on the line, but not in the same way that it is for a closer.

Dennis Eckersley is one of the few successful starting pitchers who became a relief pitcher. His was a brilliant transition—giving him a second Hall-Of-Fame type career as a reliever who never threw the ball over the middle of the plate.

© Steve Babineau

## *Set-Up Guys*

The evolution began with starters, developed closers, and finally settled in the middle—on the set-up guys. As baseball expanded and the talent diluted, starting pitchers weren't capable of pitching deep into the game until it was the closer's turn. So, there had to be a way to get from a five- or six-inning starting pitcher to a closer.

Teams began looking for guys who could go one or two innings without the pressure of closing a game. Good arms. That's what characterizes all set-up guys.

The role of the set-up guy is to get through the seventh or eighth inning, when it's getting to be crunch time. But there is still time, and not as much pressure.

### The Difference Between Closing and Setting Up

The closer is the last stand. He pitches to the heart of the lineup or the best pinch hitters off the bench. He comes in when the other team's back is up against the wall and they give it all they have. The closer knows that if he blows it, his team loses.

On the other hand, if a set-up guy blows it, his team still has a last chance to get to *their closer*.

# Long Relief

Often, the last guy to make a pitching staff is a long reliever. This pitcher was once a starter or has future aspirations to be one. But for now, his job is to mop things up.

That's right. Sometimes starting pitchers get off to a bad start, and then they get worse. Hey, it happens to all of us. But it doesn't always happen. So, on a good team, a long reliever could go ten games or more before seeing any action. This can be a tough role, because he has to be ready game after game. And you are always hoping you don't have to use him. If he comes in, your team is probably already in some kind of early trouble. His job is simple. Stop the bleeding and hold the game right where it

is. His job is to give your offense some time to figure a way to scratch back into the game.

# Left-Handed Specialists

There are certain left-handed hitters that scare you. And even though you may have a great right-handed set-up man in the game, you see this left-handed hitter (let's call him Ken Griffey Jr.) and you think he may have an advantage on your right-handed closer. That's how it works, because when the ball comes from the same side of the mound the batter stands on, it's harder to see. Statistics back this up.

Teams bring in a left-handed pitcher to face this one batter because the odds are better for a left-handed pitcher facing a left-handed batter than they are if teams use a right-handed pitcher.

Sometimes, left-handed specialists throw only one pitch. If that's all it takes, that's a job well done. They are always saved for key situations late in the game, because after that one batter, they are usually removed. Their specific job is to get out superstar left-handed batters late in the game.

# Pitching – Fastballs and Curveballs

## CHAPTER SEVENTEEN

**HITTING IS NOT EASY** and pitchers do their best to make it confusing, too. Pitchers come to the mound with arsenals—fastballs, change-ups, curveballs, sliders, screwballs, knuckleballs, and forkballs. Each pitch is different on different days, depending how the pitcher feels. Pitchers can throw these pitches *anywhere*.

It is hard to master more than a two or three of these pitches, but it is worth learning about all of them. Before any pitcher worries about a specific pitch, he must first master the mechanics of a good pitching motion.

## It Starts with Balance

In baseball, balance is key and that is especially true in pitching. If you don't have good balance, it is difficult to get any kind of drive and

momentum going toward home plate. Without balance, the pitch will lack velocity and it will be nearly impossible to get the ball to the location you want.

# Starting a Basic Windup

Even though I am left-handed, I will explain the basic windup from the perspective of a right-handed pitcher because most pitchers are right-handed.

You start with both feet on the mound, facing home plate. Then while continuing to face home plate, you step back with your left foot. As you step back with your left foot, turn your right foot parallel with the mound (on the rubber) so that you have a base to push off of.

## The Leg Kick and Stride

Once your right foot is turned on the rubber, it is time for your leg kick. You take your left leg from behind you and you lift it off the ground while turning your body sideways to home plate. The leg kick is simple: just bring your knee up. There are a million variations on this theme, but the idea is to simply get some momentum.

The key is balance. When I am teaching kids, I always tell them that they should be able to stop their windup right in the middle of their leg kick and balance. The size of a leg kick is a matter of personal preference. A leg kick can be high or low. You should use whatever is comfortable, but

you should be able to stop a leg kick, balance on one leg, and then make the transition toward home plate.

The size of your leg kick is a matter of personal preference. Mine is a short kick and Dennis Eckersley used to almost drop his head below his knee. Both work fine.

As you transition out of your leg kick, you want to drive toward home plate and step in a direct line to where you are throwing the ball—whether that is right down the middle, the inside corner, or the outside corner. The better your foot is in line with where you are throwing, the easier it is to keep your upper body square and going toward your target.

## *Your Hands: Following the Path of Your Leg*

Every pitcher moves his hands differently. I don't move much because I believe that the less I move, the less chance I have of something breaking down in my windup.

Some guys bring their hands up over their heads or have a big leg kick. So much movement seems like a waste to me. But what do I know? It works for some guys.

## *Throwing and Finishing*

Some players throw overhand, others throw three-quarters overhand, and still others throw side arm or even the old submarine style. The throw has to do with comfort and performance. If you experiment, you find what is comfortable and what works. That's how all pitchers find their style.

Some guys are power guys, bringing it straight overhand and simply over-powering the batter with a huge leg drive and a power form. Watch Roger Clemens and you will see a guy who throws like this.

**TIPS**

**TOM'S**

Everybody is different. So, how do you find a natural motion? Well, go out to the outfield and fling the ball as naturally as you can to the infield. There you go. That's your natural throwing motion. Pitching is just a refinement of that movement.

Other guys are wiry. Orel Hershiser is a relatively small, thin pitcher who turns his body into a precise rubbery instrument. He seems to fling the ball, and yet he is effective because he puts it where he wants it.

After pitching, the pitcher wants to finish in a position that allows him to be another infielder. Once the pitcher lets go of the ball, he is an infielder.

## *The Stretch*

When there are runners on base, a pitcher wants to get the ball to home plate as quickly as possible. He also wants to be able to throw to the other bases to keep the runner from wandering too far toward the next base. Thus, he uses the stretch.

The stretch is like the windup, except you start parallel to the mound rather than on top of it. In other words, a right-handed pitcher would start facing third base rather than facing home plate. A left-handed pitcher faces first base.

From the stretch, you gain speed in getting the ball to the plate, although you actually throw the ball a little slower. Or, if you throw it at the same speed, you have to work harder because you don't get the natural leg drive and momentum that you get from a normal windup. For me, that's not true. I don't use my leg kick but I am still able to use my hips. I have to work harder, but I can still achieve my velocity.

### *The Mechanics That Concern Me—Leg Kick and Landing Foot*

Sometimes, things break down and the results show it.

If my leg kick is too short, I tend to rush toward home plate and I open up. If my leg kick is too long, I am dragging, my arm is dragging, and my pitches are up in the strike zone.

Mechanically, the other key to my pitching is my landing foot. Some pitchers land on their toes. I land on my heel. The key for me is to pay attention to how my foot lands and make sure it lands straight on. I know if I land a little closed or a little open compared to straight on. I use "straight on" as a reference point.

I think most pitchers would agree that it helps to have a pitching coach. There are so many things going through your mind that another set of eyes helps. Of course, the better you get the more you want to recognize things yourself rather than relying on someone else. No one knows you like you do.

# *Fastball*

The fastball is the fastest pitch. It is the pitch you throw the hardest and the one that you can usually rely on most for strikes.

There are two kinds of fastballs:

- **Four-Seam Fastball:** This tends to be a little straighter and a little faster, and it is a little bit easier to control. Hold the ball across the

horseshoe of the seams of the ball so that the tips of your first two fingers are on the seams.

- **Two-Seam Fastball:** This pitch drops and moves. But make no mistake, this is still a fastball. Hold the ball with your first two fingers between the seams. If you want more movement, hold your fingers together just barely touching the seams. If you hold your fingers apart on the seams, you will get less movement but more control.

# *Curveball*

A curve doesn't just curve. It drops.

Think of it this way on a clock: a right-handed curveball drops from about one o'clock to about seven o'clock. It has a break, and it falls. Generally, it is thrown about 10 to 15 mph slower than a fastball.

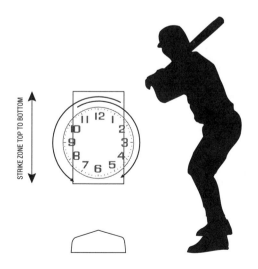

A curveball from a right-hander breaks from about one o'clock to seven o'clock. And from a left-hander like myself, it breaks from eleven o'clock to five o'clock.

There are a lot of different grips for a curveball, but generally you hold one of the seams. I would do it one of two ways:

- Hold the ball between the seams like my two-seam fastball—touching both seams.

- Starting with my two-seam fastball grip, I would slide my hand over the seam that was touching my middle finger and hold this seam with my index finger—straddling that seam.

The key to a curveball is turning the wrist. You DO NOT want to turn your elbow. Instead, you come out of your fastball motion and then turn the ball at the end. I simply turn my wrist and throw my fingers down. Doing this makes the ball spin. The harder you spin it, the harder it breaks.

**TIPS**

**TOM'S**

I do not recommend that a young pitcher try to learn to throw a curveball. Many people teaching the curve don't know how to teach it and a lot of kids end up hurting their elbows. There is a great risk of injury for a young, growing pitcher.

It takes a while to learn to control a curveball—learning how much spin creates what kind of a break. Generally, when you are throwing a breaking ball, you want to throw it higher because it is going to break down.

If it breaks too much, it goes into the dirt and it is difficult for a catcher to handle. If it doesn't break it is a slower pitch up in the strike zone. The next sound you generally hear is a home run being smacked.

# Slider

The slider works like the curveball—only different.

It turns more than it drops. It drops only a little, but it moves across the plane of the plate causing the batter to hit the ball on a different part of his bat than he plans. It moves from side to side a little faster than a curveball and a little slower than a fastball.

It is thrown with the same grip as the curveball. But unlike the curveball, instead of throwing your fingers down, you roll your wrist and throw your fingers to the side.

Think about the clock again. A slider breaks across—from nine o'clock to three o'clock for a right-hander. A left-hander's slider would break the other way.

# Change-Up

If you can mess with a hitter's timing you can mess with his swing. The best weapon you can develop is a change-up to go with a fastball.

A change-up works because it looks exactly like a fastball, but it is slower. You throw it the exact same way. It moves the same. It just comes in

slower. If a batter is waiting for a change-up, he can probably see it and clobber it. Use the change-up to confuse a batter who is expecting a fastball. If he is ready to hit a fastball and the pitch comes in too slow, he swings too soon and fouls it, or even misses.

This pitch works because of the grip.

There are a few different kinds of change-up grips but the most common is the circle change. Make the OK sign with your hand by putting your thumb and index finger together to make a circle. Then put the baseball in your palm and grip it with your other three fingers.

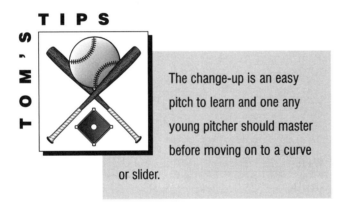

**TIPS**

**TOM'S**

The change-up is an easy pitch to learn and one any young pitcher should master before moving on to a curve or slider.

The change-up is thrown from the outside three fingers using the two-seam or the four-seam fastball grip. The index finger is only used for balance. Though thrown just like a fastball, the circle change grip gives the slower change-up pitch a built-in change of speed.

# Forkball

If you spread your index finger and middle finger as far apart as you can, and put a baseball between them, you have a forkball grip. It is a slower pitch that some pitchers use as their change-up. When thrown, the ball does not rotate; it tumbles and falls.

# Split-Fingered Fastball

Instead of pushing the ball far into the gap between your fingers like the forkball, a split-fingered grip spreads your fingers around the ball. This pitch has a downward spin and moves more than a change-up.

# Screwball

To pitch a screwball, turn your wrist the opposite direction from a curveball when throwing. It is a very unnatural motion but it makes the ball spin away from the hitter. It's a great weapon, but it really wears on your arm.

# Knuckleball

I don't know much about a knuckleball except what I hear and see. The ball does not rotate. It does not do what anyone tells it to do. It has a mind of its own.

For a pitcher, the knuckleball is the last resort. You turn to it when nothing works anymore and you need to do something drastic to save your career. You swallow your pride and learn to throw this slow, non-spinning version of aimed unpredictability. For some guys, it works. For most guys, the thought of throwing a knuckleball eighty times a game and taking their chances with it is scary to even think about.

The grip is in the name. The knuckles are on the ball. Some guys put them on the laces, others on the leather. Some use their fingers and almost push it like a shot put.

The knuckleball is unpredictable. It might drop six inches. It might go left or right. It might dance a little. Or, if a knuckleball pitcher does not have good movement that day, it might come in slow and flat—like a target.

# The Mindset of a Cy Young Pitcher

CHAPTER EIGHTEEN

**I *KNOW WHAT I DO WELL***, so I plan to keep doing it until someone beats me at it. Then I'll think about trying something different. Until then, I'll keep throwing outside.

There are other approaches. Some pitchers attack a batter's weakness instead of pitching where they pitch best. It is a subtle yet significant difference. I have spent years learning the art of pitching and learning what I do well. I don't care if what I do well is also the batter's strength. I'll still do it because it is *my* strength.

Discovering that strength has been a key to my success.

# *Learning about Myself*

Baseball was just work. I always had talent, like a lot of guys, but I learned that talent alone wasn't going to get me into the big leagues. I needed a repertoire and a plan. In the minors, I had a fastball, a curveball, and a slider. Then, after my rookie year in the majors, I knew I needed a change-up, too.

The saying is true: You learn from failure more than you learn from success.

So you start making changes, and you start succeeding.

Through trial and error I found my way. I recognized my successes and failures and I built on that knowledge. I realized that I needed success in order to survive, so I made changes. I found success and stuck with it; success built on success and pretty soon it just snowballed.

## *Why I Quit Throwing Curveballs*

Ideally, every pitcher would like to have four great pitches. The reality that faced me after more than ten years in the big leagues is that you are not going to have four great pitches. You are probably going to have two good ones and one or two mediocre ones. Usually, you want to be a jack of all trades.

Until 1998, I tried to throw four pitches. Finally, I gave up the curveball because it wasn't doing me any good and I wasn't getting any better. So I thought about my core philosophy of doing what I do best. I don't do

curveballs best. Therefore, I no longer throw curveballs. I decided to concentrate more on my slider to make this pitch better.

# Pride Leads to Work

*Are you serious?* That's the question all pitchers ask themselves. If they are serious about becoming good pitchers, they have to sacrifice and work, and they have to be disciplined.

If you think you are in good shape, you need to be in better shape. It is always about doing a little bit more. You want to be prepared in every way, in every aspect, for every situation.

You work to get to the major leagues. You work harder to stay here. Plenty of guys have had a cup of coffee in the majors, but takes more to stick around and find success.

It takes work, physical and mental work, day after day and year after year, to stick around. I have been pitching in the big leagues for eleven years now and I know I have more to learn. I know I am in good shape and I am prepared, yet I always strive for more.

I always use an internal challenge to prove myself right or wrong. If

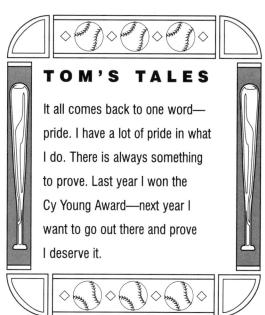

**TOM'S TALES**

It all comes back to one word—pride. I have a lot of pride in what I do. There is always something to prove. Last year I won the Cy Young Award—next year I want to go out there and prove I deserve it.

I have a bad year, I want to prove I am better than that. If I have a great year, I want to prove it was no fluke.

**Working hard is a key to my success.**

© Chris Hamilton, Atlanta, GA

I never want to go to the mound unprepared—whether it is spring training or the seventh game of the World Series. I don't want to embarrass myself, and there is always a chance for that to happen in baseball. Of course, no matter your preparation, you will have a bad game from time to time. The less it happens, the easier it is to deal with. Pride is about one thing—being ready. You should always be prepared to play the next game at peak level.

# Positive Thinking and Focus

Attitude makes a difference.

I know. If you tell yourself *don't do something* the chances increase by a million percent that you will do it.

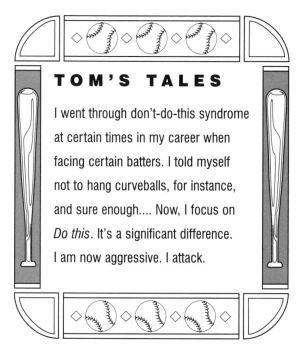

## TOM'S TALES

I went through don't-do-this syndrome at certain times in my career when facing certain batters. I told myself not to hang curveballs, for instance, and sure enough.... Now, I focus on *Do this*. It's a significant difference. I am now aggressive. I attack.

I am fortunate because I have always been a pretty strong person mentally. I have been able to deal with stuff. That comes from my parents, I guess. I have always looked at things two ways:

1. I have a responsibility. I don't care what else is going on.

2. This is an escape from the trials and tribulations of everyday life. If I can take two hours out of the day to get away, then I want to have some fun. Baseball is always fun.

## *Starting with Strike One*

So, how do I pitch? Well, I start with strike one.

That's the pitch that counts the most until strike three. In a baseball game, strike one counts more. Of course, in a strikeout, strike three is prettier, but a strikeout is a mere one twenty-seventh of half a baseball game. Strike one always sets up something, which sometimes includes strike three.

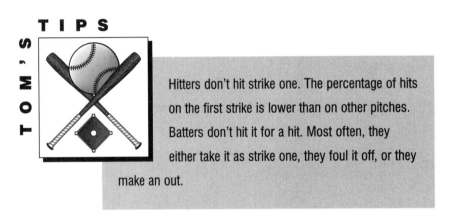

Hitters don't hit strike one. The percentage of hits on the first strike is lower than on other pitches. Batters don't hit it for a hit. Most often, they either take it as strike one, they foul it off, or they make an out.

The percentages are with you on strike one, so you may as well throw it. After that, it goes downhill.

## *Working the Count*

You don't always get strike one. Sometimes, you miss, which results in ball one. Ball one is a hitter's count because he thinks you want to throw a strike rather than going down 2-0. He figures he is probably going to swing and thinks, *Well, he still might try to get me to chase a pitch.* And he is right.

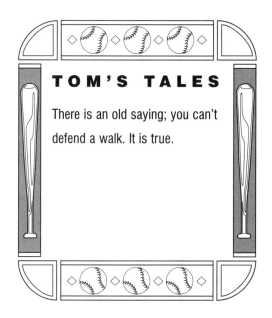

**TOM'S TALES**

There is an old saying; you can't defend a walk. It is true.

Pitchers know that the more you work ahead in the count the more it opens up your options. You can't exactly expect a good batter to chase a pitch on a 3-0 count. It just doesn't happen. Good batters are smart. They will make you prove yourself.

An at-bat is a battle of wills. Batters want one thing. Pitchers want another.

And somebody wins.

As the at-bat develops, advantages are gained or lost. If a pitcher gets strike one and then strike two, he is in a position to waste a pitch. The batter knows it. But the batter also thinks *What if the pitcher throws another strike? Then what?* So the batter has to stand there waiting for *anything*.

If the pitch is 0-2, the pitcher's mindset is *Do not give up a hit*; the hitter's mindset is *Do not take strike three*. And so the pitcher usually throws a ball. But not always. There are two sides to this story.

There are two sides to the entire count. As much as you want strike one, there are benefits to pitching ball one, sometimes. On a ball one count,

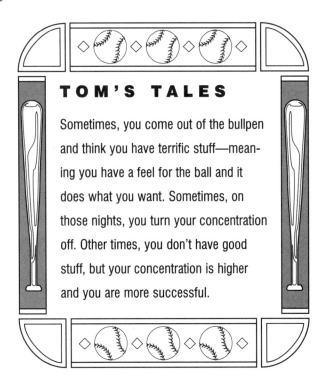

## TOM'S TALES

Sometimes, you come out of the bullpen and think you have terrific stuff—meaning you have a feel for the ball and it does what you want. Sometimes, on those nights, you turn your concentration off. Other times, you don't have good stuff, but your concentration is higher and you are more successful.

most pitchers choose a fastball because that is the one pitch they are sure they can get over the plate.

But I know a hitter is going to hit in a fastball count, and I know I can throw a good fastball there. But I also know I can throw a change-up. So if he starts to look for a change-up, I might throw a fastball. All I have to do is mix it up a little. Then he doesn't know what is coming.

As the count develops, the pitcher or batter has an advantage, depending on who is ahead. If the count gets to 2-0, this is a hitter's count because he figures you have to throw a strike. If it becomes 3-0 or 3-1, it is also in his favor. The situation will dictate how aggressive a hitter will be. If, for instance, the count is 3-1 and there is a base open, the pitcher might not give in to the batter. If, however, the bases are loaded, the batter knows the pitcher must throw a strike or walk home a run, so the batter knows he will get something to hit. He swings out of his shoes.

## Working Both Sides of the Plate

One criticism of my pitching is that I pitch on the outside corner and I don't use the inside corner enough. This approach is not recommended because a right-handed hitter will crowd the plate in anticipation because he knows I am not going to pitch on the inside.

I do pitch inside every once in a while to plant a seed that I just might do it again—maybe once or twice an inning, or maybe not for a couple of innings.

**T I P S**

**T O M ' S**

You hear good hitters talk about giving up one side of the plate. That means they decide that if the pitcher throws it on one side of the plate, they can't hit it; so they aren't going to swing. But if the pitcher throws it where they are looking, they aren't going to miss.

Of course, batters remember. If I get a guy out in the first inning, he remembers how I did it when he comes back up, say, in the fourth inning. So, I might try something different. Let's say in the first inning I had two strikes and then I threw him a fastball inside to get strike three. He remembers that.

What I do depends on the batter. I know better than to try to get the upper echelon hitters out the same way every time, because they are too good and they will figure it out.

## *Working a Batting Order*

Pitchers think about more than one batter at a time. Before an inning, I am well aware of who is coming up and the scenario I am facing. But when I am facing a hitter, I am only thinking about that batter. I focus on the job at hand.

But there is no question that if you know the top of the order is coming up, you don't want the leadoff guy to get on base. If he does, that opens up the steal and the hit and run, and it puts the power guys batting next in a position to drive in some runs.

Some teams' entire batting order can take you deep. On other teams, only batters 3, 4, and 5 can take you deep. So on any given day against any given team, you figure out how they could beat you and eliminate those possibilities.

Sometimes you are beaten. Imagine facing Mark McGwire or Tony Gwynn with two men on base and only one out. Geez, that's a situation you don't want to be in. During the course of a nine-inning game, you will have your ups and downs in terms of concentration. When you face Mark McGwire or Tony Gwynn, your concentration must be 100 percent; you know theirs is. In fact, in this situation, you are often apt to give up an intentional walk. You face certain guys and think, *I am not going to let him beat me.*

## Going for a Strikeout

Strikeouts often happen; sometimes you go for them. If there is a runner on third base with nobody out, you need a strikeout. But usually it is easier to force a hitter to ground out than it is to get a strikeout.

## Working Fast

There are a number of reasons for a pitcher to work fast. First, it helps his fielders get into a rhythm. If the fielders are standing around waiting and waiting for the pitch, they are not as ready to make a play. But if the ball is pitched soon after the pitcher gets it, the fielders are ready because the action is quick.

Also, working fast disrupts a hitter. Hitters would always like a little more time between pitches to adjust, make themselves comfortable, and get ready to hit. The pitcher wants to rush that timing and make the hitter uncomfortable.

## *Dealing with Pressure*

I was nervous when I pitched in my first big league game. I was nervous when I pitched on Opening Day and at the All-Star Game—in fact, at any game, I always get butterflies.

But before a big game, it *is* different. There are so many people watching and you have a lot to lose if you lose. You can climb a mountain of anxiety quickly if you let yourself.

Channeling the anxiety is the key. For me, it is a matter of getting out there and throwing the first couple of pitches. I want to settle in. If I finish the first inning unscathed, I get a good feeling about the game. Then the nervousness wears off and it is a baseball game.

When I have some success I become confident, which leads to more success. When I get on a roll, I am not fighting myself. I am letting my abilities and concentration take over. I feel that I'm moving well and following my game plan.

# A Thinking Person's Game

## PART SIX

**PREPARATION IS A KEY PART OF BASEBALL** because it is a game of decisions. On the field, players make decisions. On the bench, the manager and coaches make decisions. All must be prepared for any occurrence. When a decision is made, even if it seems to be right, it can go wrong. In the end, the right decision is the one that works.

Countless decisions are made throughout a baseball season, and some will be wrong; so fans will have plenty of opportunities to second-guess the manager. Fans from now until forever will argue about what happened.

In this final part, I explain some basic baseball logic and introduce a baseball team's staff—the manager, coaches, and trainers.

# The Job of a Manager

## CHAPTER NINETEEN

**I** HAVE HEARD MANAGERS SAY THAT THEY MAKE **300** DECISIONS A GAME. In the National League, where there is no designated hitter, that may be true.

But a manager does more than make in-game decisions. He sets the tone. The manager of a baseball team is the leader and the general—the personality who rules. He inspires and, yes, he makes decisions. He alone has the ability to use pure force of personality and—even if that force is understated—to drive the team forward. The manager can also dominate the team with negative emotional outbursts that will characterize the club. Negative emotional outbursts by teams often show up in the loss column. But, it all depends on the chemistry between the team and the manager. Some emotional managers have been very successful.

## Setting the Rules and the Tone

Every manager has his own set of rules and those rules will dictate how his team plays. The key for a manager is to know the strengths and weaknesses of his players and then make his rules work for each one. The manager must unite all the players to work together toward a common goal—winning.

TOM'S TIPS

There is no one style of managing that always works, because if there were one such style obviously everybody would use it. And then it couldn't work every time because somebody always has to lose.

From personal experience, I know that Bobby's rules work. Bobby Cox, our manager, sets the tone. We all get to the field on time. We wear our uniforms the right way. We don't wear earrings and non-baseball items on the field. We wear our hats the right way. On Bobby Cox's team, we are baseball players—*professional* baseball players.

An emotional up-and-down manager will produce an emotional up-and-down ball club. This is especially dangerous for a young ball club. If an emotional manager is in charge of a young team prone to mistakes, and if he flies off the handle every time he witnesses a mistake, the ball club will be full of guys who are afraid to make mistakes. That's not a winning

formula. A young ball club will thrive much better under a more patient manager who is also a good teacher. Of course, the emotional manager could rub veterans the wrong way, too. Older players won't have a lot of patience with a manager who angers at every little mistake.

Labels are not 100 percent accurate. An emotional manager can often be a good teacher, and a manager known as a teacher could be a hot-tempered guy. Legends grow as stories are told over and over again.

## My Three Managers

I have played for three managers in the major leagues:

- Chuck Tanner was a rah-rah everything-is-OK kind of guy. His attitude was, we'll get them tomorrow.

- Russ Nixon was a more emotional manager who wore his emotions on his sleeves.

- Bobby Cox is a mix of everything. He is very emotional about the game, but he doesn't let that carry over to his players. If you make a mistake, he will talk to you and tell you how you should have done it. It ends there. He doesn't talk down to you and he doesn't talk down about you in the press. He has respect for his players, and his players have enormous respect for him.

Bobby Cox sets the tone for our team. He helps us keep the emotion out of it so we can always make intelligent, rational decisions.

© Chris Hamilton, Atlanta, GA

# *Picking the Team—*
# *General Manager (GM) and Manager*

A good organization communicates well from top to bottom. One of the most crucial links is between the manager and the general manager. In a well-run organization, the manager and the general manager talk to each other about the team.

The manager might express his concern about an area in which the team is lacking. The general manager will respond by saying something like, "Well, this is who I think we can get. But this is who I have to trade for him. Do you think it's worth it?"

There is give and take, but ultimately the GM makes the decisions concerning trades and free agency. However, if a manager is adamant about

not wanting a certain player on his team, the GM will probably not pick up that player. But the GM will not always listen to the manager.

Although the manager may know everything going on in his clubhouse, the general manager knows the intricacies of the budget and how to make a trade happen. Communication is the key.

## *The Roster*

A team's roster is a numbers game. It differs between leagues, though every team has twenty-five players.

In the National League, the pitcher hits, so the team is a more likely to use a pinch hitter for the pitcher. Therefore, most teams in the National League will carry eleven pitchers, while most in the American League will only carry ten pitchers.

- A National League team has 11 pitchers = 11.

- The team has eight starters 11 + 8 = 19.

- This leaves six positions.

- Some teams have three catchers, most only have two. That means one extra catcher 19 + 1 = 20.

Teams either have three extra infielders and two extra outfielders, or vice versa. It all depends on the versatility of the players involved. In most cases, teams have two extra outfielders and three extra infielders.

In the backup infield, teams first need a strong defensive shortstop because this is such an important position. They need a player who can back up second base, shortstop, and third base decently. A backup first baseman is also required.

In the outfield, a regular outfielder or a backup outfielder must be able to play center field. After that, outfielders must have some pop in their bat. Outfielders are offensive players.

# _Writing the Batting Order_

A batting order is an attack strategy.

When a manager takes a look at his players on the field, he decides how to send them up to the plate. Basic baseball strategy calls for running an all-lefty batting order up against a right-handed pitcher and an all-righty batting order up against a left-handed pitcher. Of course, relief pitchers are always a possibility, so teams like a good mix of strong left-handed and right-handed batters. Often, they use a few platoon substitutions based on which arm that day's opposing pitcher throws with.

After considering the opposing team's pitcher, managers like to have certain kinds of hitters in specific slots in the batting order.

- The leadoff hitter probably has the best speed on the team. He is a good hitter with a good eye to get walks. When he is on base, he is a dangerous base stealer.

- The #2 hitter is similar to the leadoff hitter but he probably will not hit as well or have as much speed. He will handle the bat well enough to bunt or execute the hit and run.

**T I P S**

**T O M ' S**

In the American League, the designated hitter often bats in the #3, #4 or #5 spot. After all, he is in the batting order specifically to hit. He plays no defense.

- The #3 hitter is probably the best all-around hitter on the team. He will have a good average, probably hits for power, and drives in a lot of runs.

- The #4 hitter is the cleanup hitter—meaning that if the first three batters get on base, it's his job to clean up the bases. He is a power hitter who drives in runs and is a *presence* in the lineup.

**T I P S**

**T O M ' S**

Managers try to put a good hitter behind another good hitter in the batting order. The reason is to "protect" the first good hitter. In other words, if the #4 hitter is great but the #5 hitter is only average, a pitcher may walk the #4 guy to get to the #5 guy. But, if the #5 guy causes just as much worry, then the pitcher will just go ahead and pitch to the #4 guy rather than put an extra runner on base for the just-as-dangerous #5 hitter.

• The #5 hitter is another power hitter who often bats from the opposite side of the plate as the #4 hitter.

• The #6 hitter is often a younger hitter who may someday blossom into a #3, #4 or #5 hitter. Or he is a good hitter but not a great one. He often has adequate numbers in both his batting average and power.

• The #7 hitter (in the National League) is often one of your defensive specialists who hits some and has some speed. In the American League, the #7 hitter is similar to the #6 hitter.

• The #8 hitter is a lesser hitter. At the very least, he should be able to work the count and get on base with two outs and nobody on. If he does, your #9 hitter can make the last out and you can start your next inning with the top of the order. (If your #9 hitter doesn't make an out, then there are two men on base for the top of the order.)

• The #9 hitter (in the National League) is the pitcher. The #9 hitter in the American League often has a fairly good average and speed to set things up for the top of the order.

# Setting the Rotation

Our team is probably a little bit different than most teams. For instance, here is how Bobby Cox has chosen our opening day pitcher in recent years.

Whoever won the previous year's Cy Young Award gets to start opening day.

© Chris Hamilton, Atlanta, GA

**Our rotation of Cy Young Award winners makes it easy for Bobby Cox to pick his starters.**

Bobby Cox has a bit of luxury in that way.

Most teams struggle to find one #1 starter. On the Atlanta Braves there are three of us—Greg Maddux, John Smoltz, and myself. In 1997, Danny Neagle was on our staff and he is certainly good enough to be a #1 pitcher as well. On our current pitching staff, there isn't pressure on any one of us because, in a sense, each of us is "The Guy."

**TIPS**

**TOM'S**

The choice of a #1 pitcher is relevant to the talent of the pitchers on the staff. Some guys are #3 on one staff and could be #1 on other staffs. This works in reverse, too.

- The #1 guy is the pitcher that a team relies on to win a lot of games and, especially, to turn around losing streaks. In an ideal world, he is a twenty-game winner. On most teams he is a workhorse, expected to pitch 220 or so innings, win a lot of games, and provide leadership.

- The #2 and #3 pitchers are expected to be workhorses as well—pitching 200 innings and winning games. In other words, you want them to win more than they lose.

- The #4 and #5 pitchers are often young players teams are trying to develop by letting them eat as many innings as possible. Wins, of course, are always nice, but teams are happy simply if these two pitchers win more than they lose.

Often, after the starting pitcher is chosen, the rotation order boils down to mixing left-handed pitchers and right-handed pitchers. Ideally, a team has a righty followed by a lefty followed by a righty followed by a lefty, etc. Most teams don't live in an ideal world. Most teams are searching for left-handers and adequate #4 and #5 starters.

## Using the Bullpen

The bullpen starts where it ends—with the closer. The closer comes in and shuts down games. As the manager chooses his rotation, he also decides on a closer because this position is as important—if not more so—than the starting pitcher.

The closer is the anchor, the ace of the bullpen. He has an attitude and finishes up the game.

But sometimes, it takes another pitcher to get from the starter to the closer. This is when a manager relies on the rest of his bullpen.

© Chris Hamilton, Atlanta, GA

A key part of baseball strategy for a manager is knowing when to make a change, and when not to make a change.

Usually, he will have two lefties. One will be a long-relief lefty ready to go two or three innings or more. The other guy will be the specialist—and I mean specialist. One left-handed pitcher in every good bullpen is an expert. His job is to come in and get out the best left-handed hitter on the other team.

The bullpen will have two right-handed relievers as well. One is a set-up man who plays one inning near the end of the game.

The bullpen needs at least one long reliever—a pitcher who can come into a bad situation and stop the damage. He pitches when the pitcher has trouble early in a game. He is supposed to stop the other team from

scoring so that his team has a chance to catch up. Managers hope they don't have to use this guy a lot.

## Going by or Against "The Book"

In baseball strategy there is a standard way of playing that is often called "going by the book." Going by the book is strategically and statistically safe. In other words, if a left-handed pitcher is on the mound and you want to put in a pinch hitter, the book says you should put in a right-handed pinch hitter because, statistically, right-handed hitters do better against left-handed pitchers than left-handed hitters.

But sometimes a manager knows that his best left-handed pinch hitter has been successful against this particular guy. Or maybe he has a gut feeling that his lefty is right for this particular situation.

These moves are very important and often make the difference in a game. A manager has to "read" his players and know, for instance, how long to leave a starting pitcher in the game. He needs to think about that particular game and how pulling a pitcher too early or too late will effect that pitcher's confidence.

## It's Still Up To the Players

In the end, a manager can only win if his players produce on the field. A manager *does* make a difference, but he is limited because he doesn't pitch, play the field, or swing a bat.

# Coaches, Signals, Trainers, and Support

## CHAPTER TWENTY

**THE MANAGER IS THE BIG-PICTURE ADMINISTRATOR**—the guy making the decisions and setting the tone for the team. The coaches do the grunt work and give input to the manager. Coaches are generally the ones throwing at batting practice, hitting at infield and outfield practice, and helping the players prepare. Preparation is a key. In addition, the conditioning coach helps with preparation and the trainers help when players are injured.

## *Bench Coach*

The bench coach is the manager's right-hand man. Typically, a bench coach has a lot of experience—often he is a former manager. He has a few formal duties such as posting the batting order and keeping track of it, but his most important role is informal—a listener. The bench coach talks to

the manager during a game. He shares his ideas with the manager, who sits in the dugout during the game wondering *should we do this or should we do that?* Often the manager thinks out loud and the bench coach will tell him if his gut feeling makes sense. The bench coach must be knowledgeable and the manager must trust him.

The bench coach also manages the batting order. He writes out the lineup and posts it in the dugout; every inning he posts who is leading off and who made the last out for both clubs. He scratches out names and writes in new ones.

## *Batting Coach*

Batters are not perfect. They are always striving to be better, more comfortable, and more confident. The batting coach is another set of eyes. A batting coach is on the

© Chris Hamilton, Atlanta, GA

Andres Galarraga is a great example of how coaching helps. He started out his career with some great years in Montreal. Then he got hurt, went to St. Louis and struggled. When he landed with the Colorado Rockies and manager Don Baylor, his career took off to new heights. Part of the reason is this crazy open stance he started using—at the suggestion of Baylor.

outside looking in at the batter in his stance—he can see things that the batter sometimes is not aware of.

The basics of hitting are the same for all hitters—balance, seeing the ball, and getting the bat through the zone. But all hitters are different and a good batting coach works with hitters individually.

Batting coaches watch the mechanics of each batter and watch how the opposition pitches to each batter. The batter might come back to the bench and say something like, *That pitch was right down the middle, how did I miss it?* And the batting coach might answer, *You pulled off it a little*, or *You didn't get started soon enough*, or *Your hips flew over*. He will share what he noticed.

Or the batter might come to the bench and say, *I just can't quite figure out how this guy is trying to get me out. I can't figure out his pattern.* And the batting coach will say something like, *Your first time up, he did this and this. Then, your second time up he did this and this. Your next time up, look for ____*. A good batting coach simply knows his hitters and knows how opposing pitchers try to get them out.

## Pitching Coach

Pitching is a subtle art. The pitcher has a lot to think about, so every team has a pitching coach to provide an extra set of eyes and advice. A pitching coach actively helps a pitcher with mechanics and game management.

## Working on Mechanics

If a pitcher is on his game, the pitching coach will spend some time with him to help him maintain his good form. If a pitcher is struggling, the pitching coach will probably spend more time looking for subtle changes the pitcher can make in his delivery. Generally, a struggling pitcher has a mechanical problem. It could be as simple as turning too much or not turning enough; or maybe his elbow has dropped just a hair. It is often very subtle.

It helps to be around a coach who knows you and can suggest things that have worked in the past: *Remember when this happened before and we did this? Let's try it again.*

## Game Management

A pitching coach will help a pitcher plot a strategy and keep the pitcher on course during the game. They may talk in the dugout. Sometimes, when there is trouble, the pitching coach will be sent to the mound to have a conference with the pitcher.

Sometimes, a pitcher just needs a break in the action to settle back down.

© Chris Hamilton, Atlanta, GA

During the game, the job of a pitching coach is to keep an eye on mechanics. Sometimes he will come to the mound to talk about game strategy: *Hey, you've got a base open, how do you feel about walking this guy to get to the next batter?*

His involvement goes even deeper. He has to get in the pitcher's head and figure out what makes him work. When things start to unravel, a pitcher's mind speeds to 100 mph and the pitching coach realizes somebody better call "time out." The pitching coach refocuses the pitcher and helps him move beyond his anger at the situation.

## When Leo Mazzone Visited Me

In 1992, our pitching coach, Leo Mazzone, found a way to get in my head and helped me find a way to eliminate a big problem. That year, I had trouble getting through the first inning. Generally, if I got through the first inning I settled down and pitched fine. But the first inning had caused me problems. I don't know if I was nervous, or what. Leo visited me during the first inning of a number of games. We talked about mechanics but never about that specific problem. During the first inning of a game in San Diego I was having trouble. Leo nonchalantly walked out to the mound and asked if my arm hurt. "No," I told him, my arm didn't hurt. He replied, "Well, if your arm doesn't hurt why don't you start acting like you can pitch or I'll find someone who can." He came out to get me angry and he succeeded. My first inning jitters disappeared.

### *High-Tech Help*

Baseball is now a game of information. Every pitch is charted. This means that the results of every pitch—whether it is a foul ball, straight back, or to left field or right field—it is recorded. Every ball put in play is charted on a graph and it shows me who hit what pitch and where they hit it. It can be helpful. It can also be overkill. Generally, I look at these charts when I am playing a particular team. If there are two or three guys who have great numbers against me, I will study it further. I am not worried about the guys I am successful against.

In addition, I have access to video. Once again, this can be overkill. I use video at the beginning of the season to re-familiarize myself with certain teams and hitters. Usually I avoid video unless I run into problems with my mechanics and I can't figure it out. In that case, I can go to our staff and have them focus on my windup from certain angles. For instance, they will tap into the home plate TV feed and tape the game from there. When I really have problems, I compare what I am doing now with a videotape of my performance in Game 6 of the 1995 World Series. That was my career game—I was *on* everything.

## *First Base Coach*

The first base coach is in charge of any runner on his way to first base or any runner on first base. If the batter puts the ball in play, the first base coach will yell, *Dig it out! Dig it out!* He will try to inform the runner when it is going to be a close bang-bang type of play.

If there is an overthrow on a ground ball in the infield, he helps the runner locate the ball so he can decide whether or not to go to second.

© Chris Hamilton, Atlanta, GA

**When you get to first base, the first base coach reminds you of the situation and tells you what to look out for.**

Generally, once the runner reaches first base, the coach will remind the runner of the situation: *OK, there's one out. Watch for the line drive, don't get doubled up. And watch out, this guy's got a good pick-off move.* The situation dictates the conversation. With a runner on first, the first base coach will help with signals. If there is a hit and run signal or a bunt signal, the first baseman will often not cover the bag so the coach can tell the runner the play. (Keep reading for more on signals.)

A first base coach is also keeping an eye out for the pitcher's pick-off move to first base.

## *Third Base Coach and Signals*

The third base coach is a traffic cop and a signal man. He makes the critical decision whether to send a runner from third base to home, and he also relays signals from the manager to the batter and the runners.

### *The Signals*

A lot happens during the season, so most baseball signals are simple, and most are kept for the entire season. There are usually signals for a bunt, hit and run, steal, and squeeze.

These plays do not happen very often, yet if you watch the third base coach, he is busy making decoy signals all the time. Most of what he does means nothing. He throws so many signals to confuse the other team.

The signals could be as simple as:

- Steal—touch nose

- Hit and Run—grab belt buckle

- Bunt—touch chin

- Squeeze—touch ear

Often, teams disguise their signals with an indicator—a signal that must be given before the real signal. So, if the indicator is rubbing your arm, you would rub your arm before touching your nose to signal a steal. Without the indicator first, a nose touch is just a nose touch. With the indicator, it is a signal to steal.

## TOM'S TIPS

Coaches, more than players, are the ones trying to steal the signals. The players are usually paying attention to the action directly on the field.

## The Decision

To send the runner, or not to send the runner? Third base coaches decide.

A third base coach is generally in charge of a runner once the runner has passed first base and is headed for second. But sometimes the runner can see the play better. If he is on first and the ball is hit to left center, he can see where the ball is going and make his own decision. But if it is hit to right center, he has to look to the third base coach who will help him decide whether to stay at second or run to third.

If the runner is on his way to third, the third base coach must make the crucial on-the-spot decision of whether to send a runner home.

**A third base coach has to make a quick decision whether to be cautious or tell the runner to slide.**

© Chris Hamilton, Atlanta, GA

He could wave his hands around to signal the runner to go; he could hold both hands up in the air and tell the runner to stay; or he could put both hands down to indicate to the runner to expect a close play and slide!

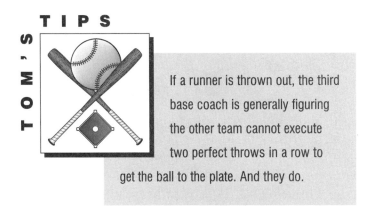

**TIPS**

If a runner is thrown out, the third base coach is generally figuring the other team cannot execute two perfect throws in a row to get the ball to the plate. And they do.

When a third base coach has to make a decision, he slides down the line toward home to get a better angle on the runner and on the ball in the outfield. He moves down the line to give his runner a couple more steps before he has to decide, because he can still see him. He buys himself some time by finding a better angle and calculating the arm strength of the outfielder and the infielder involved in the potential relay.

## Strength and Conditioning Coach

The strength and conditioning coach enhances a player's chances of staying on the field. He works with each player individually.

Those who play every day usually don't lift weights a lot. Some will lift on an off-day or when they have a day off. Others don't want any part of the weight room once the season starts. The strength and conditioning coach helps each player find a program that works for him.

Pitchers generally do more work than regular players. Pitching is cardio-vascular, so pitchers run more than other players. You drive your leg every time you throw a pitch.

### TOM'S TALES

In the heat of the summer when it is 100 degrees, if you have a rough inning, you come out after the inning almost withered. These types of games are where conditioning really comes into play.

## *Training in the Winter*

In the off season, I am trying to get stronger. I am not necessarily trying to get bigger, but my weight training in the winter is drastically different than it is during the season. In the winter, for instance, I do more free weights in order to build muscle so that when the season starts I'm ready.

When the season starts, I use Nautilus-type machines with low weights and heavy repetition in order to maintain my strength.

# *The Trainers*

Players hope to never see the trainers. But, chances are, they will sometime. That's just the nature of baseball.

The trainer is who you see when it hurts. It is comforting to know that the trainer is knowledgeable and willing to put in the necessary time to treat what is bothering you—usually with specific exercises, icing, or time in the whirlpool. Often, it takes a lot of time. That can mean working with the same trainer two or three times a day. If the player doesn't show up, he delays his own recovery.

## When to See the Trainer

After the first game of spring training, no one is playing 100 percent and something always hurts—that's how it is.

Other times you *know* something is wrong; or at least you know when someone should check it out. As a left-handed pitcher, I am always aware of my left arm. I have been pitching long enough to know that I have a bit of tendonitis. It doesn't feel good but I know what it is and I know I can pitch without hurting myself. On the other hand, if I felt something different, I would not hesitate to consult the trainer to assess the condition of my arm.

# Baseball Strategy

## CHAPTER TWENTY-ONE

**BASEBALL STRATEGY IS IMPORTANT TO EVERY GAME.** There are games without a hit and run, without a bunt, without double switches, and without pinch hitters. But generally, one of those will come up. Even if they don't, the manager thought about these possibilities—particularly in the National League.

## *The Difference Between Leagues*

There are fewer managerial moves in the American League compared to the National League. That's not a knock on the managers. In the American League managers don't have to worry about a pitcher coming up to bat in the middle of a rally. Pitchers don't bat in the American League.

In the American League, for instance, a pitcher on a team losing 5-0 will keep pitching in the sixth inning. In the same circumstance in the National League, the pitcher will be taken out of the game so the manager can pinch hit for the pitcher. In the American League, a designated hitter hits for the pitcher.

The American League is known as the home run league. It has more power hitters and smaller ballparks because teams don't need to manufacture runs as much as they do in the National League. In the American League, managers rely on the three-run homer. In the National League, managers encourage runners to steal bases, bunt, or go for a hit and run.

## Steals

A key weapon for any team is the steal because it turns one base run into two. The greatest base stealers consider the situation before they run.

First and foremost, the runner must consider the guy on the mound. If the pitcher is quick, most likely the runner won't take a chance because stealing demands a jump. If the pitcher has a great move to the base and a quick delivery to home, it is more difficult to get a good jump. After thinking about the pitcher, the runner considers the catcher's arm and the game situation.

In some ways, the threat of a steal is as big a weapon as a steal. Anytime there is a runner on base who draws the attention of the pitcher, the pitcher is less effective. If a pitcher is not giving a hitter 100 percent of his attention he is not 100 percent effective.

The game situation often dictates whether a runner will steal or not. For instance, a runner will steal late in the game if his run will mean something. So, if you are tied or down by one in the seventh inning you will steal a base to get into scoring position, because if you score you tie the game or take the lead. If you are down by two, you will not risk the steal because you need two runs to tie. Your run will not change the outcome of the game.

## Stealing Second, Third, and Home

The key in all steals is the jump, and the key to a jump is to read the pitcher and know the instant he decides to go home with the pitch.

Most runners steal second base because more runners reach first base than second or third. But most runners say that it is easier to steal third than it is to steal second. Usually, runners can get a bigger lead at second base.

Runners most often steal home on the back end of a double steal in which a runner from first steals second, draws a throw, and then the runner on third steals home.

# Hit and Run

The theory of the hit and run is to guess which infielder will cover second and then hit the ball into that hole. However, teams have scouting reports on batters and they will try to cover the field according to the batter's tendencies in such situations.

Teams use the hit and run when they want to manufacture runs and don't have a power hitter at bat. Typically, you would not hit and run with a forty-home run guy up.

The hit and run is really more of a run and hit. The runner takes off. The batter protects him by hitting the ball. If he doesn't hit the ball, the runner will be out because the runner actually waits a little longer than he would on a steal.

© Chris Hamilton, Atlanta, GA

The hit and run is a timing play that is used to move runners forward.

A typical hit and run situation develops when the team at-bat has a runner on first base who isn't fast enough to steal, and the batter is not powerful but has great bat control.

Usually when the hit and run is called for, the ball is hit. If it is not hit, the runner will often be out "stealing" by fifteen feet. When the hit and run is called for, the runner must be protected by the batter. If a batter can hit a ball to a specific place on the field, it's very helpful. Someone like Tony Gwynn can do that. Most batters can't. Instead, most batters go up with a specific plan to hit the ball on the ground.

At certain counts, managers are more likely to call a hit and run. Teams will hit and run on 1-0, 2-1, and 3-1 because the pitcher will usually try to pitch a strike.

Sometimes, pitchers will "pitch out," meaning they throw the ball outside the strike zone to make it easy for a catcher to throw out a runner, and impossible for a batter to hit the ball.

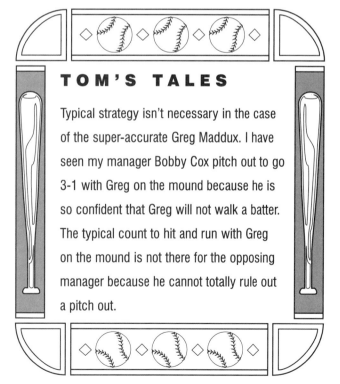

**TOM'S TALES**

Typical strategy isn't necessary in the case of the super-accurate Greg Maddux. I have seen my manager Bobby Cox pitch out to go 3-1 with Greg on the mound because he is so confident that Greg will not walk a batter. The typical count to hit and run with Greg on the mound is not there for the opposing manager because he cannot totally rule out a pitch out.

# Pinch Hit

Each team generally has a #1 pinch hitter. The manager calls on him when the game is on the line. In the American League, pinch hitters are used almost exclusively in late innings. The #1 guy is always saved for the end. In the National League, teams use a pinch hitter more often because the pitcher is in the batting order. Pitchers generally can't hit as well as professional hitters and there are only so many chances to catch up.

But the #1 guy is always saved. He is not necessarily saved for the ninth inning because you may not have a chance to tie the game in the ninth. In the seventh inning, for instance, if the situation is right, the best pinch hitter on the team will be called in to bat for the pitcher, the weak-hitting infielder, or whomever the manager picks.

## Being a Pinch Hitter

I have heard guys talk about how much more difficult it is to be a pinch hitter than it is to be in the game. If you are a pinch hitter, you spend your time preparing for one at-bat that may not even come. You try to pay attention to the game, and you try to be ready when your team needs you. Some guys are better at it than others. You can count on them when situations arise late in the game.

# Pinch Runner

I was a pinch runner in my younger days. It was nerve-wracking. You are put on base to run for a slower player. But so many things can go wrong. You can get picked off, thrown out, or miss a base; or you could make a bad judgment and try to steal a base when you shouldn't. A pinch runner comes into the game fresh and has to make game-speed decisions.

I remember one game I came into as a pinch runner. It was late in the game, the ninth inning. We were sacrifice bunting—giving up the batter to advance the runner, me—but the bunt went in the air. And I had to judge it. I wasn't sure if the pitcher was going to get it or not. I froze. I took one step and then leaned the wrong way. The pitcher dove, caught the ball, and threw to first. I had no chance to get back. This was very embarrassing. We were down by a run in the ninth inning, and the next thing I knew, I was on the bench with two outs.

# Bunt

The bunt is usually a sacrifice, meaning the batter is essentially giving himself up so that the runner can move forward a base. You force the defense to make a hard play and give the runner advance warning that you are going to bunt so he can get a quick start. If it works, the defense can only throw the runner out at first.

Certain fast runners are exceptional bunters who will, on occasion, try to bunt themselves onto first base. If he can outrun the throw, it is a tremen-

dous weapon because it forces the third baseman to play in, which gives the batter room to hit.

© Chris Hamilton, Atlanta, GA

**A well-executed bunt is a good way to advance runners and even get on base.**

If there is a runner on first base and you are trying to bunt, you will bunt the ball toward first base because the first baseman has to hold the runner. When he charges, he has a longer way to go than the third baseman, who will play in on the grass of the infield when he anticipates a bunt.

If there are runners on first and second base, you will generally try to bunt the ball to third base—hard enough to get past the pitcher but soft enough to force the third baseman to charge the ball and vacate his base. Then his only play will be at first base.

## Squeeze Bunt

A squeeze bunt happens when the batter bunts the ball and the runner steals home at the same time.

The timing of the squeeze bunt must be executed perfectly to work, and when the timing is right it works nine out of ten times. It is a surprise play, and the execution doesn't have to be perfect. The batter just has to get the ball on the ground. The key is the timing. The batter squares himself as late as possible because he doesn't want to give anything away.

**TIPS**

**TOM'S**

As a pitcher, if the guy squares too early and you see it is a squeeze bunt happening, try to throw the ball high and inside. This should either force the batter to get out of the way or perhaps force him to bunt the ball in the air for an easy pop-up double play.

# Intentional Walk

Sometimes, a pitcher will throw four straight high outside pitches to intentionally walk a batter. Why? Some guys are dangerous. Mark McGwire and Sammy Sosa, for instance, are big power hitters who can send any pitch to the moon. You decide to put them on base and let the next guy try to beat you. Sure, the next guy after a power hitter is usually a good hitter as well. But not all guys can hit the ball to the moon.

A more common scenario for walking a batter is when there is a base open and you want to set up a double play. If, for instance, there are runners on second and third with one out and the #7 hitter is coming up, you may walk him—not because you are particularly fearful of that hitter— but because if you load the bases you create a force out at any base.

A pitcher might not walk the batter if there is an open base, two outs, and the pitcher is ninth in the batting order and waiting to hit. In this situation, he may want to try to get the #8 hitter to swing so the pitcher leads off the next inning. This works because the batter will cooperate. He doesn't want to send the pitcher up to bat with the bases loaded, so he tries to get a base hit and will expand his strike zone a little.

The intentional walk is called when the catcher stands and puts his hand outside the strike zone. Just because it is called, though, doesn't mean that the pitcher has to throw balls. He can throw strikes.

And the batter can swing.

## Double Switch

In the National League, when a manager wants to remove a pitcher in the middle of an inning, sometimes he will make two changes instead of one.

The double switch buys a pitcher some pitching time.

The manager will change the pitcher and one fielder. The pitcher will bat in the fielder's spot and the fielder will bat for the pitcher. The reason is simple. If the pitcher is due to bat early in the next inning, the manager doesn't want to pinch hit for him because he just brought him into the game. So, he makes two switches and adjusts his batting order. The position chosen for the double switch will be a player not due to bat until seventh or eighth in the following inning. Then the manager hopes the pitcher pitches well and justifies this move.

# *Index*

# WIN A TRIP TO BASEBALL FANTASY CAMP!

Be a big-leaguer for a week on us! Just fill out this entry form and tell us your baseball fantasy in 50 words or less, and you can win a trip to the ATLANTA BRAVES DREAM WEEK™ held at the Braves Spring Training Camp in Disney's Wide World of Sports Complex. The 5-day action-packed extended weekend includes this and more:

- 5 days/4 nights accommodations...
  *(Double occupancy, private room optional)*.
- Round-trip team flights from Atlanta, Georgia...
- Group transportation...
- Your own authentic Braves uniform *(home white and batting jersey)* and head to toe accessories to keep!
- Custom Dream Week™ warm-up jacket.
- Continental breakfasts and lunches in the Clubhouse.
- Daily practice sessions with your Braves heroes.
- Professional coaching in hitting, fielding, pitching and game fundamentals.
- Current minor league managers to assist you with extra practice.
- Your own Clubhouse locker.
- Daily big-league games.
- All playing equipment *(bring your own glove and cleats)*.
- Personal Clubhouse Staff and Professional Trainers.
- Opening night Welcome Reception.
- Saturday evening Awards Cocktail Party and Dinner.

## PLUS THESE BONUSES

**Your Own Baseball Cards with Your Own Photos and Stats**

**Happy Hours and "Bull sessions" with the Pros**

*and much, much more to make your dream come true!*

Enclose this entry form ***plus*** your baseball fantasy in 50 words or fewer. Good luck!

Name_____

Address _____

City _____ State _____ Zip code _____

Mail to: *Baseball For Everybody Dream Week™ Contest*
c/o Chandler House Press, 335 Chandler St., Worcester, MA 01602

**All entries must be postmarked no later than 10/1/99. Entrants must be 30 years old or older and in good health. Chandler House Press will announce a winner by Nov. 1, 1999.**

# *Baseball For Everybody Contest*
# *Official Rules*

1. No purchase necessary to enter.

2. Complete an Official Entry Form with your name, address, and daytime telephone number and include the following materials:

   *Essay:* Print or type an original essay, no more than fifty **[50]** words, describing your baseball fantasy.

   All entries must be your original work and must not have won any other award or been submitted to or published by any other publication.

3. Mail completed entry and materials, first class, to: Baseball for Everybody Dream Week™ Contest, c/o Chandler House Press, 335 Chandler Street, Worcester, MA 01602. All entries must be **_received_** by October 1, 1999. One entry per person, family or household.

4. *Selection of winner:* Claire Cousineau Smith, Director of Retail Sales and Marketing, will review and judge all essays. All judging will be based on originality, 50 percent; creativity, 20 percent; and enthusiasm, 30 percent. The judge's decisions are final. For the name of the prize winner, send a self-addressed stamped envelope between November 15, 1999 and January 31, 2000 to "Winner's List," Baseball for Everybody Dream Week™ Contest at the address set forth in no. 3 above.

5. No mechanically reproduced, incomplete, or illegible entries will be accepted. All entries become the property of Chandler House Press and Dream Week™ as Sponsors, and may be used for purposes of promotion, except where prohibited by law. Sponsors will not be responsible for lost, late, or misdirected mail, mail with insufficient postage, or for the return of any entry. No correspondence will be answered.

6. Contest open to residents, age 30 or older and in good health, of the 48 contiguous United States. Employees (and members of the their immediate families) of Sponsors and their respective subsidiaries, affiliates and advertising and promotion agencies are not eligible. All taxes are the sole responsibility of the winner. Void where prohibited by law. No substitution, transfer, or cash redemption of the prize is permitted.

7. Each potential winner will be required to execute a Declaration of Eligibility and a Release certifying that the winner's submission is an original work and has not been previously published; that all Contest Rules have been complied with; that the winner release Sponsors of all liability, including but not limited to personal injury or property damage, relating in any way to acceptance or use of the prize; that Sponsors (and anyone Sponsors may authorize) may use the winner's name, photograph, or other likeness, biographical information, and statements concerning the contest, the contest entry or the Sponsors, without compensation, for purposes of advertising, promotion, and merchandising (except where prohibited by law), and that the winner grants all rights in his/her entry to Sponsors, including the right to edit, publish and copyright it.

8. Potential winner will be notified by mail on or about November 1, 1999. The Declaration of Eligibility and Releases must be returned within 14 days of notification or an alternate winner may be selected.

9. One prize consisting of the following will be awarded:

   Atlanta Braves Dream Week™ package for February 2-6, 2000 *Details of package found on reverse.*

Winner is responsible for all transportation and arrangements between the winner's home and Atlanta, Georgia. Once awarded, this prize has no cash value.